Ivana Straska

CONFIDENT ME

With Confidence and Solid Self-Esteem

By Ivana Straska

 England

Confident Me - With Confidence and Solid Self-Esteem

All rights reserved. No parts of this book may be reproduced, scanned or distributed in any printed or electronic form without the written permission of the author. Please do not participate in or encourage piracy of copyrighted material in violation of the author's rights. Purchase only authorized edition.

Neither the author nor the publisher is engaged in rendering professional advice or services to the individual reader. Information in this book is intended to educate and is not to substitute consulting with medical professionals. All matters regarding your health require medical supervision. Neither the author nor the publisher shall be liable or responsible for any loss or damage allegedly arising from any information or suggestion in this book.

First edition

ISBN 978-1-9998266-5-9

Graphic design by Chris Gill for MC World Enterprise

Copyright © 2018 Ivana Straska

Published by IVANA INTERNATIONAL, England

> Building self-confidence requires an understanding of self-values and beliefs. This book helps to banish self-defeating habits and build solid self-esteem. The reader learns to mindfully create a positive self-image and bring self-esteem in line with feelings and actions.

PREFACE

Solid self-esteem is not tangible but is something that people need to smoothly move through life and do it with joy. Self-esteem is a core psychological asset allowing the utilization of skills and potential. It is a personal concept of values, feelings and actions. The good thing about self-esteem is that nobody is born with low or high esteem. Almost anyone can build a solid self-esteem.

Through life experience, people learn to think and feel someway about themselves. In self-reflection, they assess behaviour, feelings and compare them with their values. Self-esteem evolves from moment to moment by valuations and actions. The problems with self-esteem rise from what people validate and believe. Based on their beliefs, they compare themselves, and when they aren't the person they wish to be, their self-esteem goes down. To have a solid self-esteem, people have to assess personal actions in harmony with their values.

Whether someone has solid self-esteem depends on whether they live their values, whatever these values might be. When a self-esteem concept is built upon good values, people are able to grow good feelings towards themselves. Along with good values, mindfully developed self-esteem aids to remove underlined fears and conflicts. Solid self-esteem works as psychological immunity. It protects an individual's strengths and allows personal adequacy. Building self-esteem requires an understanding of values and effective actions.

The goal of this book is to help the reader build solid self-esteem based on good values and enforce positive feelings about the person they are. The following pages provide a useful and comprehensive strategy to do it. The reader will learn:

- to understand the values incorporated in self-esteem;
- to modify values of self-concept to stop self-depreciation;
- how to bring personal values in line with actions to raise self-esteem;
- to sensibly see oneself in a larger perspective;
- to understand a positive self-image;
- to change self-defeating habits eroding self-esteem;
- to stop focusing on groundless problems decreasing self-esteem;
- to control negative thinking wearing down self-esteem;
- to develop confidence growing self-esteem;
- to develop caring attitude towards self;
- mindfulness to stop being caught up in reactions;
- to remove irrational sense of isolation and inadequacy;
- finding comfort in personal imperfection and flaws.

TABLE OF CONTENTS

Introduction		vi
Check Your Self-Esteem		ix
1	**Addressing Your Beliefs**	**4**
	1.1 Thoughts Are Only Thoughts	4
	1.2 Beliefs Are Thoughts	7
2	**Finding Your Self Worth**	**11**
	2.1 Self-Worthiness	11
	2.2 Wise Focus	15
3	**Giving Your Self Credit**	**21**
	3.1 Interpretation of Failing	21
	3.2 Creating Positive Self-Image	26
	3.3 Negative Experience	30
4	**Recognizing Destructive Thoughts**	**34**
	4.1 Acknowledge Your Qualities	34
	4.2 The Positive Mind	37
5	**Self-Love**	**43**
	5.1 Personal Privileges	43
	5.2 Small Dose of Narcissism	49
	5.3 Demonstration of Qualities	52
6	**Importance of Self-Expression**	**55**
	6.1 Assertive Expression	55
	6.2 Impact of Body Language	58
	6.3 Healthy Relationships	61
7	**Good Qualities**	**64**
	7.1 Self-Compassion	64
	7.2 Shifting Your Fixation	69
	7.3 Therapeutic Focus	73
8	**Continue Building**	**78**
	8.1 Through Thoughts and Feelings	78
	8.2 Being Non-Judgemental	81
9	**Learning New Strategies**	**86**
	9.1 Using Visualization	88
	9.2 Mindfulness to Raise Self-Esteem	94
10	**Cherish Qualities**	**97**
	10.1 Towards Self-Acceptance	97
	10.2 Growing Confidence	100

11	**Decisions Affect Self-Esteem**	**106**
	11.1 Know the Principles	106
	11.2 Balancing Your Decisions	110
	11.3 Areas of Happiness	112
12	**Maintain The Positive Mindset**	**116**
	12.1 Remember Mindfulness	116
	12.2 Remain Strategic	121
13	**Sum it Up**	**124**
	13.1 Back to Self-Assessment	124
	13.2 Don't Forget	128
About the Author		**130**

What is the purpose of this book?

To help the reader understand why they should work on their self-esteem, I have to take them back to my work. When working with clients, based on studies and observations, I found that inaccurate thinking about oneself is the centre of most problems. I could produce almost an immediate effect when pointing out the client's thinking errors and their wrong focus. The concentration on the present and offered alternatives nearly instantaneously brings progress. When engaging this approach, people become aware and able to change. They can leave negativity and shift their feelings.

This book brings encouraging outcomes to a spectrum of problems as it builds self-esteem upon realistic and good values. It provides a foundation for the practise of positive mindset and behaviour to advance towards a confident experience. This book guides the reader to reset unconstructive thinking that triggers a domino effect distorting social life. They focus on positive change and behaviour to develop solid self-esteem.

Why is self-esteem so important?

Building self-esteem is crucial. When people love themselves, they make a better life. They create happier relationships when feeling loved and supported, and being able to offer love and support in return. They easily adjust or find a fulfilling career. Someone with solid self-esteem experiences good feelings. They believe they are worthy of love, appreciation, happiness and success. They can recognize their good qualities and generally strive for a happy and successful life.

Low self-esteem makes many things difficult and it affects different people in different means. Someone has low self-esteem in specific situations, others largely feel and think low about themselves. Low self-esteem is potentially dangerous and it links to mental health issues and poor relationships. Individuals with low self-esteem blame themselves for things that aren't their fault. They underestimate their abilities and lack confidence. They are unfair on themselves and they expect things to go wrong regardless of the circumstances and actions. They might be too critical and harsh as they don't believe in themselves.

What is positive esteem?

A self-concept is a spectrum of thoughts, beliefs, values and self-assessments. It is the backbone of self-esteem. People have to know that their self-concept as personal worthiness is based on the evaluation of its standards. If there is a conflict between their values and actions, they experience self-rejection. A self-concept consisting of realistic and good values allows acceptance and building solid self-esteem.

How should the reader work with this book?

Working through this book as a whole will provide the fullest knowledge and opportunities to practise all the reader can learn. Some readers might want to jump to chapters that are important to them and they can freely do it. However, they shouldn't forget that they can always return to the full book at any time.

In the pages I distinguish a few sections:

Author's comment   Reader's thinking

Reader's writing   Examples

All these parts visually differ from each other and they are equally important. Writing sections provide sufficient space and the reader should write directly in the book.

Handwriting is a cognitive exercise and it allows better access to one's feelings and thinking. It helps the development of new neurological connections in the brain. Writing thoughts into words gives them more tangible form and also it becomes the reader's valuable resource.

The book provides QR codes taking the reader to additional information and practice such as relaxation, meditation, guided visualization, worksheets and much more. The reader is encouraged to use these free sources.

 This QR code take the reader to awareness of mental wellness.

Questionnaire

In order to build self-esteem, you should understand how to create and maintain it. The following pages will discuss what impacts self-esteem and what could be done to develop solid self-esteem. Before you start, you should honestly reflect on your current self-esteem; how you value yourself and how you feel about the person you are..

Genuinely complete the questionnaire:

1. Do you believe that building healthy self-esteem is in or out of your control?

    Yes, it is in my control   No, it is not in my control

2. How often do you believe in yourself?

| Most of time | Often | Occassionally | Rarely | Never |

3. How often do you feel confident in your abilities?

| Most of time | Often | Occassionally | Rarely | Never |

4. How often do you worry about what other people think about you?

| Most of time | Often | Occassionally | Rarely | Never |

5. How often do you halt your expression of thoughts and feelings?

| Most of time | Often | Occassionally | Rarely | Never |

6. How often do you feel hopelessness and fear of retaliation?

| Most of time | Often | Occassionally | Rarely | Never |

7. How often can you find truth in criticism?

| Most of time | Often | Occassionally | Rarely | Never |

8. How often do you focus on problem-solving?

Most of time   Often   Occassionally   Rarely   Never

9. Do you worry about rejection or being alone?

Yes   No

10. Do you worry about conflicts?

Yes   No

11. Can you read the minds of others?

Yes   No

12. Are you a perfectionist?

Yes   No

13. Do you worry about disclosing your true feelings and thoughts?

Yes   No

14. Do you believe you must help when others feel upset?

Yes   No

15. Do you think you should be always in control of emotions?

Yes   No

16. Do you think you should be always happy and desired?

Yes   No

17. Do you think people should be as you expect them to be?

Yes   No

18. Do you worry about failure?

Yes   No

Confident Me

check your self-esteem continued...

19. Is it wrong to get frustrated?
    Yes   No

20. Do you worry others would find your flaws?
    Yes   No

21. Are you sarcastic or cynical?
    Yes   No

22. Do you want others to think you are perfect?
    Yes   No

23. Do you counterattack when others attack you?
    Yes   No

24. Do you think you should feel only positive emotions?
    Yes   No

25. Do you think problems are caused by others?
    Yes   No

26. Is your attitude respectful?
    Yes   No

27. Do you acknowledge other people's feelings?
    Yes   No

28. Do you express your feelings and thoughts?
    Yes   No

29. Can you find common grounds when someone disagrees with your ideas?
    Yes   No

30. Do you believe everyone is accountable for their own feelings?
    Yes   No

The questionnaire reveals the way of thinking that impacts self-esteem. People who frequently think in negative and unrealistic ways about who they are end up targeting their qualities and personality. The questions disclose beliefs that embrace how people interpret happenings. These beliefs impact the understanding of actions of other people, expectations and values. Someone who frequently thinks negatively about the person they are often dislike themselves. They experience a conflict between who they are and who they wish to be.

Feeling negative about a variety of situations is linked to how people think and feel about themselves. This impacts their actions and choices. They might act in self-defeating ways, avoid, quit or resist change. These actions have a negative influence not only on self-esteem but on their life. People might worry with no reason to or avoid risks that would be healthy for them. Low self-esteem can cause people to try and control what they can't, pay attention to irrelevant things, or they might waste their energy by trying to fix what they can't fix.

The most important thing is to acknowledge that people can change their self-esteem. They can develop balanced thinking, be positive and realistic, and create positive self-esteem. This is an achievable goal for anyone who wants to do it.

Confident Me

CONFIDENT ME

With Confidence and Solid Self-Esteem

By Ivana Straska

Confident Me

1.1 Thoughts Are Only Thoughts

F. D. Roosevelt said that people are not prisoners of their fate but of their mind. Referring to the impact of thoughts on people's actions and decisions, we know that thinking is the top of what creates a personal experience. People perceive the world not only through senses but through thinking. They think between fifty to seventy thousand thoughts daily and thinking is a central lever-shifting personal experience. Sometimes people refer to self-talk which is nothing more than thinking. People learn to control their thoughts. If they fail, their thinking could act like an untrained puppy and they become trapped by their own thinking.

Self-esteem, by all means, results from how a person thinks about their personal qualities. Ways of thinking narrowly link to feelings and emotions. Thinking about oneself can be positive or negative. It can be encouraging towards good choices or it could unconstructively block beneficial behaviour. In the next pages, you will learn to understand how your self-esteem is affected by your thoughts.

To better understand the connection of thinking and feeling, you can read more.

When I am alone or doing mundane things, I want to notice what occupies my mind. I will try to pay attention to what I think about and how I think about myself. I can correct my thoughts when they are too critical, negative or harsh. Sometimes I let my judgements go wild and they create negative emotions. I want to control my thoughts that target me as a person. I want to monitor my thoughts attacking me. I can learn to think better. Doing this helps me to feel better.

write here write NOW

Response to previous:

Actions to take in order to pay attention to thinking:

1.2 Beliefs Are Thoughts

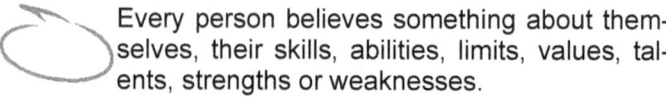 Every person believes something about themselves, their skills, abilities, limits, values, talents, strengths or weaknesses.

People develop a whole system of organized items of knowledge and ideas. Beliefs are ideas, and they start as principles that grow into internal law. They regulate an individual's decisions, choices and actions. Beliefs develop in life, and they are reinforced by experiences. Beliefs, whether they are false or correct, have resilient emotional connections. What people believe about themselves directs their other thinking.

Beliefs have functions in an individual's world. Some beliefs protect people against being hurt or feeling insecure, others provide safety or hope. This doesn't mean, however, that people hold only the beliefs they need. They preserve false beliefs through a resilient emotional network. Beliefs are inflexible thoughts that people resist to change (even if they are incorrect). People hold onto beliefs because, somehow, they work for them, and not because these beliefs are necessarily correct.

People can change their beliefs when they better understand them. Any person attaches to people, animals, objects, places, and also to ideas. When they attach to something, they can feel affection or aversion. They also feel affection to what they believe is correct. They have an aversion towards what they believe is wrong. They like what they believe in and dislike what they don't believe in. People can have aversion and affection towards beliefs about themselves. If they don't believe in themselves, they can't feel affection. And because beliefs are an individual's internal law, people comply with this law.

Beliefs are my authorities. They are my thoughts that anchor my decisions and how I interpret what happens to me. Beliefs help me to understand life, what meanings I find in my experience, what values I identify. Because the beliefs are my internal law, I can't act against them. So, if I believe I can't let go of my negative thoughts about me, I won't let them go. I won't take any action to change my negative thoughts. If I believe I can give up my negative thinking, I will do it. Once I believe in something, I commit to it. To improve my self-esteem, I change false beliefs.

When I was a child, I created "just the world beliefs". Adults wanted me to believe in predictability to feel safe. This simplification helped the child to socialize and learn about the world. It was necessary and worked well. I believed that when I did well, I would be rewarded. I believed good things happen to good people and bad things to bad people. I also believed that nice things are good. In my "just the world beliefs", I was good or bad. Things happened to me as rewards or punishments. As I grew up, I left this "just the world beliefs" behind, along with fairy tales. But I kept some beliefs about me because of my resilient emotions.

In the previous sections, the concept of beliefs was introduced. Now you will respond to what you read. Think about beliefs from a new perspective. In the following section (Reader's writing), you will write your thoughts. At first, write an overall reflection of previous paragraphs; what you know about beliefs and beliefs affecting self-esteem (for instance: This chapter pokes me to start thinking differently about me. I never paid attention to my thinking unless I was solving problems or learning something new. I don't know much about beliefs but it seems they play a big role. I never realized that beliefs impact my choices and actions...).

The second line is to select positive thoughts about the previous paragraphs (for example: This chapter helps me to start understanding my beliefs. I can learn if I hold false self-beliefs. I want to change my beliefs if they are false. I want to commit to correcting my beliefs. I can start noticing my thinking...). Lastly, try to write a few self-beliefs (for example: I believe I can't change my self-esteem, I believe I am gifted, I believe my boss likes me, I believe I am successful, I believe I am stupid, I believe my teacher hates me, I believe I can't win the next game, I believe I am ugly...).

Response to previous:

Positive thoughts:

List of beliefs:

2.1 SELF-WORTHINESS

People have a relationship with themselves. They think and feel somehow about themselves. It could be like friendship and being a carrying parent. People might be unfriendly and be their own opponents. These relationships with oneself can have various characters, and they always reflect self-values. In the next part, you will elaborate beliefs relating to how you value yourself. These are the beliefs and thoughts that target one as a person.

The values I find in myself are mirrored in my relationship with me. I want to have a good relationship with myself. I want to be like a friend to myself. I want to find values in me as my friend would do it. I want to believe that it's alright to be who I am. When I can identify values, I can give up thinking that depreciates me. I want to value myself as a unique person who has lots to offer.

Nobody sets my worthiness but me.

Self-beliefs are beliefs about personal qualities. Some self-beliefs are correct and some can be false. False and negative self-beliefs are always in the way of developing self-esteem. The person who holds onto them limits themselves and finds difficulties where they are not. The next part is about false and negative self-beliefs and how they can be changed.

Examples of negative self-beliefs: I am worthless. I am not good enough. Others are better than me. Other people have to like me. Others have to value me. I am no good.

Make a list of some self-beliefs that depreciate your values. For this part, you shouldn't question if they are right or wrong. You can start with the most apparent beliefs that you are aware of. Don't focus only on severely damaging self-beliefs but negative beliefs.

Confident Me

write here
write NOW

My negative self-beliefs:

Example

This section illustrates how you can debate your beliefs. The problematic belief of "I am not good enough" is a common belief that grown-ups maintain.

"I am not good enough" – this belief is meaningless and has to be changed. What does it mean to be good enough, how much is enough, what does "good" really mean? Good is not a measurable quantity and nobody ever knows what is good enough. This can mean a person will never be good enough, whatever they do or try. This belief makes people less worthy than others. It maintains negative feelings (hurt, distress, sad, inadequate, doubtful, uncertain, worried, anxious, insecure). It triggers self-rejection. Also, achievements and hard work briefly boost good feelings but mistakes and falls rapidly damage self-esteem. This belief asks people to prove their importance when it's not required. People who believe this battle their unworthiness and lack of acceptance.

Positive belief that replaces the negative self-belief would sound like, "I am good as I am". This maintains positive feelings (confident, fearless, inspired, caring, cheerful, relaxed) and people feel worthy. This belief positively affects self-esteem and people feel unconditionally worthy. People who think they are good as they are don't seek approval. They don't condition their acceptance. They are not crushed when they make mistakes or stay unnoticed.

2.2 WISE FOCUS

I choose to think that I am worthy. I do things that confirm that I am worthy as I am. I can write a list of my values and why I am worthy. I choose people who respect me. I want to be worthy. I don't need other people to convince me I am worthy enough because I am worthy as I am.

---

write here
write NOW

Here, you respond to the previous example. Also create a list of positive self-beliefs you are aware of.

Positive thoughts in reflection to the previous:

My positive self-beliefs:

Some beliefs that negatively influence self-esteem have no rational reasons, and they are reinforced by the wrong focus: by comparison with unachievable glamour presented by the media and social life (for instance, "I don't like my body", "My body is faulty", "I am not as attractive as I want to", "I am faulty because I am not rich", "My life is unhappy", "I have to make up to fit in", "I should be likeable", "I was born to have miserable life.")

In the current world with all the makeovers in reality shows and fashion, anyone can easily get to the point where they see themselves as not as they are but as they wish they could be or should be. Bombarded by the glamorous life of celebrities pictured in limitless happiness and abundance, anyone can feel inadequate. T.V. shows and magazines don't present a desire to live an ordinary life like the majority of people lives. An illusionary world detaches individuals from their own values. Comparison makes people think negatively about themselves and their lives. It makes them feel faulty, especially when stress is put on superficial image, appearance, wealth, success or achievements recognized by the media.

Seeing the outside world positively and seeing personal life negatively creates a lot of troubles. It can be a projected negativity preventing people from distinguishing the good things they possess, or they could possess if they take the correct actions. People fixating on the outside world overlook the good things working well for them. They might forget to appreciate personal qualities.

Perhaps I have been encouraged to compete with others but I can't continue devaluing myself. I might be self-critical because I want to be and do better. I might tell myself what I should and shouldn't. I might favour the world or others more than myself. Maybe I worry too much about what people think and say about me. I wish to change this. I want to feel safe and acknowledged. I have to accept myself. I want to see myself in a positive light. I have to stop comparing. I can change the negative perception of myself when I direct my focus on my values. I must recognize good aspects of me. I want to see myself with kindness and compassion.

---

write here / write NOW — Try to think more precisely about negative beliefs that might be enforced by your peers (family, co-workers, community) and comparison to others.

My beliefs that could negatively impact self-esteem:

Example

This section continues debating negative beliefs. The problematic belief of "I want to be liked by others" is another belief quite commonly maintained by grown-ups.

The negative belief of "I want to be liked by others" maintains low self-esteem. It makes people uncertain and inadequate. Perhaps developed through comparison and with a good intention it creates personal inadequacy. When children are reminded of how they should and shouldn't be, they may try to fit in at the cost of self-worthiness. They grow into adults while depreciating themselves. People with this belief might be worriers who are concerned about rejection. The belief of "I can like myself as I am" could replace this negative belief. When one believes they can like themselves as they are, they don't condition their acceptance. They don't belittle themselves and accept uniqueness.

My self-esteem is an integral part of personal happiness and wholeness. I build my self-esteem on human qualities. My esteem can grow from finding my values and things I can be grateful for. This helps to identify the real me. My self-esteem can branch from acceptance, kindness, compassion and gentleness. I want to be aware of my strengths and qualities.

Confident Me

write here / write NOW — Similarly, as in the previous part, try to critically think about the previous paragraphs since you did your last bit of writing.

My reflection in response to the previous part:

My positive thoughts in reflection to the previous part:

Values I can recognize in me and my life:

Here you can listen to guided imagery "Allow Good Feelings". The password is "emotions" without the quotes.

CHAPTER 3

How people interpret personal successes and failures matters a lot. Narrowly, it relates to the ways of thinking and abilities of individuals to objectively recognize circumstances affecting failures and successes. Failing to rationally acknowledge the reasons erodes self-esteem.

3.1 INTERPRETATION OF FAILING

Whether people succeed or fail, they attribute it to something. Attributes are the reasons people give for personal successes or failures. People who lack positive self-esteem are unfair to themselves and they wrongly assign attributes. For example, when they succeed, they attribute success to a lack of competition or the easiness of tasks. On the contrary, when they fail or make mistakes, they are harsh. They select themselves to be accountable for everything. They overlook circumstances that work against their possible success.

Do people give themselves the credit they deserve? Everyone has to find their answer. In the following section, you will learn about the interpretation of successes and failures. You will try to identify what may cause a misinterpretation and how to change it.

How I interpret my past, successes and failures influences my actions. The factors I consider when I identify why I failed or why I succeeded are my reasons to do or not to do something now. They fuel my motivation. When I misinterpret my mistakes, failures and successes, my self-esteem is hurt. I blame myself. I must learn to objectively identify the reasons when I fail. When I am successful, I will give credit to myself. I have to fairly distinguish my contribution and work.

People may apply irrational beliefs that work against them. Here are a few examples of negative beliefs related to failures: I don't impact the factors that contribute to my success. I can't succeed when I already failed. Failure is wrong. People who fail are wrong. I have a fear of failure. I don't try because I might be disappointed. I always fail. When low-esteem people succeed, they minimize themselves and this can be identified by their interpretation. Here are a few examples that diminish personal successes: There was nobody good to compete with. The tasks were very easy. Anybody would succeed. It was a mere coincident. The judges didn't pay attention to my mistakes.

write here / write NOW

Here, try to identify your ways of thinking when you reflect your actions and outcomes.

My thinking and how I interpret my successes and failures:

Example

Another example of negative beliefs is used to prompt your thinking to dispute your own beliefs and negative thoughts. Some grown-ups believe "Nothing that I do really matters". A belief that people don't have an impact is not true. It's false and it sabotages self-esteem. Possibly, this belief originates from minimizing personal effort or power. Although it may seem people have no control, they have limited choices of what they do. Their actions and contributions really matter. The neutral belief would sound like, "My contribution is important". It sounds positive and empowering. It doesn't deny limits. It doesn't imply outcomes as outcomes can vary. Someone who believes in their influence is strongly motivated and they act. Also, this belief allows taking healthy risks and appreciating personal impact. It inspires self-esteem.

Confident Me

write here — In this part, reflect on your understanding of this chapter so far.

My response to previous and positive thoughts:

_____

_____

_____

_____

Three positive self-beliefs:

_____

_____

_____

I take these actions to objectively interpret my successes and failures:

_____

_____

_____

_____

3.2 CREATING POSITIVE SELF-IMAGE

Habits of thinking about oneself and personal life impact how people perceive themselves and what kind of self-image they have. People believe what they can or can't do. They also believe what can or cannot happen to them. Sometimes their negative thinking targets themselves and this impacts their self-image. They might over-criticize, dwell on mistakes, focus on imperfection, ponder on their negative past or their daydreaming is their escape from reality. These mental activities impact their self-perception and expectations along with history and personality.

In this section, you will focus on expectations on how well or poorly circumstances work for or against you. In simple words, expectations can be positive or negative. For instance, if someone expects that their competition is better than they could be, they will avoid a contest (negative expectation). If someone expects that their competition is very strong but they can be prepared well enough, they would take a challenge (positive expectation). People expect from themselves, others and the world. When talking about expectations, notice personal qualities: characteristics, appearance, skills, abilities or capacities. Expectations that relate to others and the world are possibilities or conditions that a person can encounter. Negative expectations and perceptions distort self-esteem. People are bind by unfounded limits and avoidance. They don't give themselves a chance to build self-esteem.

Certainly, positive expectations that take personal contribution into account hugely impacts self-image. This comes along with constructive actions and fighting limits. It allows experiencing and taking healthy risks. It motivates and triggers choices to act. The most important thing is that you acknowledge that you can purposefully build positive expectations and perceptions as part of a solid self-image. You can personalize a statement that you can get what you expect if you act on it.

I hold a self-image. I believe what I can expect, what can happen to me and what I can do. I interpret happenings according to this image. I anticipate how well or poorly things work for me. I might find meanings in what happens, especially when the things don't go the way I wish. These meanings may result from my misinterpretation. I want to have positive expectations. If I believe I cannot do something, I am not motivated. When I believe I am inspired, I do it. I can intentionally create a positive self-image. I can have positive expectations.

Example

Here, you will continue analyzing beliefs related to negative self-image. Some examples: My father was a loser and so am I. I never achieve what I try for. My family is cursed. I can't do anything to change. Good things happen to others, not to me. I always screw up. I can't do better.

People might believe they don't deserve better. This belief sounds sour and regretful. It makes people put up with mistreatment and devaluation. A person who doesn't believe they deserve better overvalues others. They might try to meet the expectations of others at the cost of self-harm. They have different measures for themselves and others. A belief of "I can expect good things" or "I deserve _" strengthens a positive self-image. It enforces confidence and self-validation. It allows actions and self-protection.

I am worthy of a good experience. I deserve to be happy for once. I learn from negative experiences and from mistakes. I allow myself to move on. I intentionally create a positive self-image. I believe I can do things. I am willing to take healthy risks. I accept that sometimes I make wrong choices. I learn from them. I forgive myself and move on. I am worthwhile of a positive self-image. I am worthy of good things as anyone else.

Confident Me

write here
write NOW

Thoughts about positive self-image and expectations:

Three positive self-beliefs:

I take these actions to enforce positive self-image:

3.3 NEGATIVE EXPERIENCE

Some people get caught in rejection, disappointment or hurt that they experienced in the past. They overlook other positive or neutral experiences as nobody's life only has dark sides. Being trapped in the past comes at a high cost. People lose hope and they don't allow themselves to experience positive events. Dwelling on what has happened and not moving on has to be interrupted. Often, looking at the past from a wider perspective and in the context of circumstances is important. Interpretation of a negative past is crucial. Confidence that upcoming events will be different than the past is acquired by a balanced understanding. Low-esteem people might find it challenging to believe in a positive future. Negative experiences should have closure so that people can look into a bright future.

I want to have a positive attitude towards what can happen in the future. I can change how I think about my past. I can't change what happened in the past. I can change how I interpret what happened when I put it into a wider perspective. Life can be unpredictable and the future is blank. I can always control how I think. I am learning to remove myself from the midst of negativity. The now matters. I have been creating my experience.

Here you can listen to guided imagery "Let Go of the Past". The password is "emotions" without the quotes.

Confident Me

write here
write NOW

Actions to let go of negativity and the past:

Example

The negative belief of "I always miss receiving support" could be an example when people turn attention towards what they miss. They might miss support but also resist accepting help when it's available. People need to let go of this belief and replace it with something like "I can receive support", "I am open to support", "I can get support when I need it". This triggers feelings of trust and security. People don't expect it but they allow it. They recognize existing support.

Confident Me

write here / write NOW — In this part, you are encouraged to choose one negative self-belief and dispute it like in previous examples. You should finish with creating a neutral or positive belief that can replace the old (negative) belief.

My negative beliefs:

_____

_____

_____

I want to change this belief because:

_____

_____

My new (positive or neutral) belief:

_____

_____

Actions I take to enforce my new beliefs:

_____

_____

CHAPTER 4

Self-esteem consists of characteristics that people identify as important components of the person they are. People can underestimate some of their qualities. Low self-esteem can arise in specific areas or situations. Some people compensate missing qualities by overestimating their other qualities. Some people might assess all their qualities as being very low or high. For instance, perfectionism is not as good as it might sound.

4.1 ACKNOWLEDGE YOUR QUALITIES

People can learn to realistically judge their self-esteem and do it without hurting their feelings. There are a few components that create self-esteem. You could be aware of how much or how little you have to work on for your improvement. The next estimate you will do should help to direct your attention to the weak parts of self-esteem. It is important to remember that components of self-esteem are changeable. High numbers of some components can be a good sign while high numbers of other components suggest troubled self-esteem. Here is the list:

Here is the list.

acceptance	respect	reliance	control
confidence	worthiness	discipline	help
improvement	love	protection	preservation
assurance	expression	examination	importance
awareness	satisfaction	approval	criticism
pity	hatred	denial	

In the next writing, you will sensibly estimate your components of self-esteem by rating them. Put numbers 1-10 beside each component.

1 = Not at all.... 10 = A lot

COMPONENT	SCORE	COMPONENT	SCORE
Self-Acceptance		Self-Respect	
Self-Reliance		Self-Control	
Self-Confidence		Self-Worth	
Self-Discipline		Self-Help	
Self-Improvement		Self-Love	
Self-Protection		Self-Preservation	
Self-Assurance		Self-Expression	
Self-Examination		Self-Importance	
Self-Awareness		Self-Satisfaction	
Self-Approval		Self-Criticism	
Self-Pity		Self-Hatred	
Self-Denial			

I try to be realistic and honest. I can reflect what parts of my self-esteem I should improve. Building positive self-esteem comes with the awareness of my strengths and weaknesses. With effort, I can overcome weaknesses. Sometimes I have to work towards improvement. I can be optimistic. I can be confident. I can do it.

write here
write NOW

Components of self-esteem to improve:

Actions towards their improvement:

4.2 THE POSITIVE MIND

People naturally tend to worry and think negatively. They do it because their ancestors had to pay attention to threats in order to survive and they passed down DNA carrying this information. Remote ancestors also had to be aware and distinguish imagined dangers from real dangers to survive. This was also passed down through generations. In modern life, it can cause false alarms. People think "what if" and imagine bad things. Their awareness skyrockets and they consider imagined danger to be real. This can become a thinking error. False alarms and awareness trigger reactions that can consequently erode self-esteem.

In the next part, you will learn to recognize thinking errors.

Example

Here are a few categories of thinking errors affecting self-esteem. Carefully observe whether or not you can recognize your thinking errors.

Criticism
It is a thinking error when people are unfair to themselves. They might be too self-critical and harsh. This unwarranted criticism blocks their ability to objectively reflect their flaws or mistakes. They might be self-punitive for weaknesses or natural limits. When people forget to filter criticism from others, it is a thinking error. People use their subjective values to judge and their criticism might be unwarranted. People have to strain one-sided and unfair criticism. Thinking errors may cause people to misinterpret comments of others and

interpret neutral comments as ambiguous criticism. They might disregard well-intended compliments.

Measurement
Thinking errors can cause imbalanced values when they weigh negative more than positive, measure neutral events as failures, exaggerate mistakes as catastrophic. They might give credit to luck, inadequacy, circumstances and other people. They overlook and don't value personal inputs. Their self-worthiness originates in comparison with others. They measure by possession and because others are or do better in their measurement, they feel worthless.

Fears
Thinking errors come from fears and doubts. They can grow from "what if" thinking. These errors can be identified by thoughts such as: what if I am worthless? What if my feelings are less important than the feelings of others? What if I fail? What if I won't succeed? What if they won't like me? Etc. This false alarm exaggerates negative possibilities and people start believing them or act as if they are in real danger. Loss of hopes and trust originates in fear and can develop into a thinking error. Thinking errors can trigger further fear, rejection or disappointment.

Guilt and shame
People might hide their guilt and shame. Guilt and shame sometimes go hand in hand; the same action may give reasons to feelings of both shame and guilt. Shame may result from the awareness of guilt. It's a painful feeling about how people appear to others and to themselves. Shame doesn't necessarily depend on having done anything. People can feel ashamed of their weaknesses or flaws. Guilt is a feeling of responsibility or regret for

something wrong. In other words, shame relates to self and guilt to others, whether real or imagined. When guilt and shame stay unprocessed they can grow into thinking errors.

write here / *write NOW* — In reflection to the previous paragraphs, you are encouraged to write about thinking errors:

Actions I take to eliminate thinking errors:

So far, you related thinking and beliefs to self-esteem but also general beliefs about the world and others impact self-esteem. For instance, religions influence attitude towards a body, sexuality, behaviour or forms of clothing. You need overall introspection of beliefs to create balanced views. It is beyond the scope of this book to elaborate belief systems; however, awareness of values you commit to is important. The next paragraphs discuss areas of most common misconceptions. Some of them relate to values and others to behaviour. They are included in the section of examples to point how you would benefit from alternating them.

Example

Control
Everyone believes in a certain level of control they have over their life. Someone might believe they have almost no control and everything is God's will. Others might think they are helpless victims of fate. Some people believe they have complete control over everything, or they have to fight against what they don't like. Whatever the reader believes, it's important to know that nobody is in complete control or no control. Some situations might seem conclusive but people choose how they respond. The balanced thinking allows the belief in some control and giving up some control.

Fairness
People who judge every experience by its perceived fairness foster low self-esteem and negative feelings. There is almost no value of life's measurement based on fairness and unfairness. Expectations of a proof of fairness are not realistic. Unfairness is a part of life experience. If people

measure the world by fairness, they create self-induced negativity.

Changing others
Expectations that other people change when one pressures or encourages them are unachievable. These can be unrealistic beliefs that happiness and success of an individual rests on other people. This type of thinking and believing is counterproductive. People who believe they can change others beat their head against the wall. A more realistic approach would be to acknowledge a personal influence. Change is a personal decision and action.

Perfectionism
Perfectionism is a barrier to positive self-esteem. Perfectionists believe they must be correct, right or accurate. At extreme levels, they can't accept the idea that they could be wrong. They would do anything to prove their rightness at all costs. Perfectionists have to exercise beliefs that allow mediocrity and tolerate imperfection. Often, perfectionists have low self-esteem in specific areas.

Rewards and punishments
People can be trapped by their beliefs that when they try hard their effort would be rewarded. People need to accept that no matter how hard they try, sometimes it just doesn't work. At times, it doesn't matter how much people sacrifice if they don't achieve what they want or hope for. This misconception can come from their unrealistic beliefs in rewards and punishments. Hard work, struggles or sufferings are not always counterweighted with a reward. Life is not governed by this general wish.

write here / write NOW — If you identify with some misconception, you are encouraged to change your thinking. Write about it here:

Action to take to enforce change:

CHAPTER **5.1 PERSONAL PRIVILEGES**

People have some rights or privileges and you should be aware of them. Sometimes just by acknowledging the rights, you can correct beliefs eroding self-esteem. Some examples of these rights are: to say no, be treated with respect, be listened to, express opinions and feelings, receive help, make healthy choices, and not to be hurt. You can identify if your beliefs don't conflict with the human rights. Understanding and accepting rights help to remove barriers. People can develop beliefs in accordance with (human) rights to enhance self-esteem. Changing beliefs is a process and sometimes people have to convince themselves by finding the evidence for why a belief is wrong or right. Through QR code, you will be taken to learn more about how to find evidence and change.

Finding the evidence.
(Extracted from TheStrongestYou)

 *When assessing my beliefs, I try to answers to the following questions:*

- *How do I know a belief is true?*
- *What in my experience proves this belief is correct?*
- *What in my experience contradicts this belief?*
- *How does this belief impact my overall self-esteem?*
- *Why is this belief important?*
- *What good can I get from this belief?*
- *What would a loving friend (a person who cares about me) say to contradict this belief?*
- *What feelings have I attached to this belief?*

Confident Me

write here
write NOW

I believe I have these rights:

My beliefs that are in conflict with my rights:

My beliefs that confirm my rights:

It's always good to be reminded that all people are worthy and improving self-esteem is critical. Valuing someone as being worthier than others can cause a lot of trouble. People contribute differently and by their knowledge and action, they increase their values, for example, on the job market, as influencers, politicians, inventors, and so on. All this, however, comes from people's actions, knowledge or abilities, not from their values as humans. When enforcing self-esteem based on human qualities, people are valued equally. Contribution to life of others, family, friends, a community or society importantly adds to self-esteem (or erodes self-esteem when input is negative). Proportionally, by having skills and abilities, people can advance when exercising good qualities. The next paragraphs discuss sometimes neglected human aspects that can work wonders when applied to self-esteem.

Acceptance
Negative experiences are part of life. Mistakes, flaws, failures or rejections are natural. People have to learn to tolerate their own and other's imperfections. Acceptance of differences and negative experiences allow moving on. Negative experiences can be used for self-development and learning. People who accept try not to repeat the same mistakes.

Forgiveness
It is a general right to forgive and be forgiven. People with solid self-esteem can forgive. Forgiveness doesn't have to be conditioned by punishment. Forgiveness helps a forgiver to move on. Also, people have to remember forgiveness is not the same as forgetfulness or denial. People are accountable for their actions and they have to cope with consequences of wrongdoing.

Thoughts are not actions
Sometimes people consider their thoughts as facts, but they are not. If someone believes that their feelings are facts, they might be misled. Feelings and thoughts are subjective. They can be legitimate and correct. They can also be wrong and misinterpreted. Thoughts have to be distinguished from actions. Thoughts can't be judged in the same way as actions.

Be likeable
If someone believes they should like everyone or should be liked by others they are aiming for disappointment. Nobody can be liked by everybody and nobody can like everyone. People choose who they like. They decide to prefer a certain type of people, and they also can change who they like. It's important to remember that even if someone is not liked, they have the right to be respected.

No harm
Everyone has the right to be valued and treated with no harm. People are accountable for their actions, decisions and choices. People are responsible for their own health, including psychological well-being. No one can be forced to put up with mistreatment. People have the right to be accepted as they are.

Uniqueness
People have exclusive values, strengths or aspirations. Individuals have the right to show their qualities. People also have personal limits which they can try to improve. People can progress through learning and change. A lack of skills or knowledge doesn't make people worthless.

write here / write NOW — Think about human aspects of yours and how your beliefs do or don't conflict with them:

Actions to enforce my positive change:

5.2 SMALL DOSE OF NARCISSISSM

In Greek mythology, Narcissus was so proud that he disdained others and he fell in love with his reflection in the water. He forgot that it was just an image and he lost the will to live.

The term narcissism has been used by the general public to refer to selfish people who are too preoccupied with themselves or behave antisocially. A pioneer of psychoanalysis and neurologist, Sigmund Freud, brought attention to self-love as a part of survival. He referred to primary narcissism in a (positive) sense of having self-love and self-admiration; a small portion of pride and love as necessary for self-preservation.

In the next section, you will focus on components of self-esteem that are necessary for emotional safety and ability to screen out emotional harm. They are self-love, self-admiration and pride.

Here are a few ideas that you can do to activate them:

- Focus on feelings not only on appearance.
- Clarify your identity.
- Accept your imperfection.
- See personal weaknesses as a challenge to improve.
- Allow variety of feelings.
- Build self-confidence on a daily basis.
- Engage in activities that boost self-esteem.
- Remind yourself you like yourself.
- Find pride when you reach any small goal or target.
- Reward yourself for achievements.
- Gracefully accept compliments.
- Genuinely give compliments.
- Learn from others to strengthen your characteristics.
- Do the things that make you feeling productive and satisfying.
- Acknowledge your strengths.
- Practise kindness.
- Practise forgiveness.

My self-esteem can flourish when I have good thoughts and do the things that make me feel proud. I can practise a positive attitude towards what I do. I acknowledge my good qualities and strengths. I am aware of my potential. I take actions to demonstrate my strengths. I can be proud of what I do.

Raising self-esteem narrowly links with the ability to focus on the process of doing things. People with solid esteem are open to new experiences and use them as training. They don't fixate on expected results or achievements; rather, they put all their energy into a process of doing. Throughout this playfulness, they create new areas that positively influence self-esteem. Their intention is to have a pleasant experience without focusing on outcomes. A positive attitude towards what they do strengthens self-esteem.

Confident Me

 This section is very crucial as most people with low self-esteem struggle to feeli self-love, self-admiration and pride. You are asked to honestly reflect on your thoughts. If you identify a negative response, you are advised to stick here longer. You can practise previously mentioned actions to activate these feelings.

My reflection of self-admiration, self-love and pride:

Actions to take to increase self-admiration, self-love & pride:

5.3　DEMONSTRATION OF QUALITIES

Once people identify their strengths, they can find ways to demonstrate them. They should do the things that exhibit their qualities. It is important not only to acknowledge personal uniqueness but also to show it. Actions people take can validate their potential. There is no intention to look for big things or exceptional talents. People can demonstrate any abilities they possess and present any knowledge they might have. Showing abilities, skills, knowledge or interests can be natural once people acknowledge they possess them.

I do the things I enjoy. I don't have to prove my validity by achievements. I don't have to feel weak when I don't succeed. I try to be proactive and do the things that improve my self-esteem. I try to be productive and demonstrate my qualities. I might sometimes fail and failures are results of actions. I choose to take them as opportunities to progress.

When focused on a process of doing things, people become open to receive feedback. They don't worry about not meeting expectations and they can receive compliments. They allow themselves to be happy with just doing something; to be satisfied by doing things they enjoy. Being pleased with oneself creates a ground for pride and self-admiration. People can feel proud about their strengths. To raise self-esteem, they can consciously build a small dose of self-admiration.

Confident Me

I do the things that exhibit my strengths. I recognize what I am good at. I don't have to do big things to impress others. Just my joy of doing something can be rewarding. I show my skills and abilities. Sometimes I do things that other people appreciate. I accept their compliments. I receive positive responses from others. I am open to take feedback. Sometimes it can be criticism. I can cope with it positively. I acknowledge when other people have good points. This shouldn't make me feel bad. I can rationally acknowledge what others have to say about me or my actions. When I get negative feedback, I am not emotional. I rationalize it. I am gentle and kind.

 Your task is to brainstorm personal qualities you can be proud of. Don't focus on big things and take into account the small things you do or share. In the second part, you will identify specific actions you can take to demonstrate your qualities. It is important not to focus on showing off but a process of doing.

My qualities:

Three actions to demonstrate these qualities:

CHAPTER 6

Self-expression happens on two levels, verbally and non-verbally. Non-verbal communication means passing information on to others but doing it with body language and verbal communication is spoken information. Both communications include context. The next sections discuss assertive behaviour and expressions as factors influencing self-esteem. People can learn and practise verbal and non-verbal expressions to strengthen self-esteem.

6.1 ASSERTIVE EXPRESSION

Communication and self-expression can be challenging. People with low self-esteem might have difficulties to express their ideas or say no to requests. They might find it very hard to talk about feelings. They might worry that by refusing requests, they will hurt others. They might think their feelings are embarrassing and as such they are not worthy of talks. Their thinking errors (fear and what-if thinking) can create images of catastrophic outcomes.

Remember that when you negatively speak about yourself or you put yourself down, you send the wrong messages. You make yourself inferior. You can improve communication and develop assertive behaviour through practice. For some people, it is easier and others have to put more effort to learn it. It is worth a try as it can be a substantial help to self-esteem.

Assertive behaviour and communication is an expression of ideas, feelings and opinions (positive or negative) without breaking rights, personal or the other person's rights. This means that people assertively express their needs and requests while behaving respectfully and with self-respect. Assertive self-expression also means standing up for personal beliefs and sticking to them. Being assertive is the ability to establish oneself without violating other people's rights. Assertive people don't allow suppressing their rights either.

When someone openly and respectfully expresses their side, they increase the respect of others and positively contribute. People can learn not to take actions because someone puts pressure on them. They do the things because they understand and momentarily choose the best option. People become naturally more assertive as they raise self-esteem and have confidence.

Assertive behaviour also relates to respecting rights people have. Here are a few rights which you can personalize and be inspired to apply:

- Right to judge your thoughts, feelings and behaviour and be responsible for them.
- Right not to offer explanations or excuses for your behaviour.
- Right to assess your responsibility for helping others.
- Right to change your opinion.
- Right to make mistakes and be responsible for them.
- Right to admit you don't know.
- Right to be independent of others.
- Right to say you don't understand.
- Right to say you are not interested.
- Right to refuse what would jeopardize your well-being.

I am learning to be assertive. I am practising positive attitude and openness. I rehearse self-expression. I trust that with practice my expression improves. Practising assertive behaviour strengthens self-esteem.

Confident Me

write here / write NOW

You should be fairly aware of benefits when you apply assertive behaviour and expressions. In this writing, you can summarize positive thoughts:

_____

_____

_____

_____

_____

Action to be assertive:

_____

_____

_____

_____

_____

_____

6.2 IMPACT OF BODY LANGUAGE

As already mentioned, people express their feelings both through words and body language. This includes gestures, body postures, ways of moving, tone of voice and facial expressions. Part of non-verbal communication is clothing and accessories. In body language, people reflect tradition and culture. Naturally, people harmonize with like-minded people and they copy their expressions. Unconsciously, people tend to mirror those who they spend the most time with. All this manifests in behaviour and body language. Body language creates a considerable portion of the image people imprint. Studies suggest that successful people (at work or in their personal life) are better at reading body language and expressing non-verbally. People can learn to improve their understanding and expression of body talk.

Body language must be understood in a wider context. For example, a person feeling cold might cuddle up to keep warmer and this can be natural. But a person who does this during a conversation with their boss might appear as if they are in fear. People should search for harmony between how they want to come across.

Body talk can indicate a person's feelings which could be understood by the way of walking, level of eye contact or facial expression. You should know that non-verbal communication is not only a self-expression but it can also trigger your feelings. Body talk can improve feelings or it can make you feel worse. For example, a person who wants to improve confidence can practise slower, straightened out walking with their head levelled. Influential parts of body talk are the eyes and tone of voice.

You should be inspired to watch your body language and use the benefits of positive body language to your advantage.

It's always good to remember:

- Standing tall and sitting straight expresses and lifts confidence.
- Dragging feet when walking shows tiredness, laziness and boredom.
- By crossing your arms in front, it can be protective and closed off to others.
- Maintaining personal space offers comfort.
- A natural smile is a positive signal that can be inviting.
- Fidgeting sends messages of nervousness.
- Inhaling like drinking with a straw with puckered lips and slowly exhaling with open mouth (exhale has to be as twice long as inhale) relaxes the body.
- So-called v-pose or victory pose with a straightened back and pushed shoulders back while keeping head and arms up increases confidence and willpower.
- Fists and finger pointing are associated with anger.
- The voice is a powerful tool – slower speaking is taken more seriously; loud speaking can be intruding.
- Clothing is a form of self-expression.
- Grooming and taking care of body can increase self-esteem.

I practise my body language to send the correct messages. I do it to trigger the correct feelings in me. I can greet others with a smile and look them directly in the eyes to convey confidence and respect. I say my name with self-respect and confidence. I practise walking and sitting straight to feel confident. I keep my head levelled when talking to others. I learn to control my breathing. Correct breathing helps me to relax. This also helps me to better control my tone of voice and speed of speech. In tense situations when I become reactive, I can excuse myself and leave. In private spaces (toilets at work, my office) I do body exercises and breathing techniques to relax and regain control. Then I return. I am ready to continue.

write here
write NOW

Response to previous:

Action to practise non-verbal communication to improve self-esteem:

6.3 HEALTHY RELATIONSHIPS

Good relationships are important for well-being. They offer comfort and security. They enrich life like spices can make food tastier. Relationships can be battles. Fruitful relationships build upon mutual tolerance, flexibility, acceptance and plenty of attempts to do things differently when something doesn't work at first.

People bring their emotions and mental states into relationships. Once someone doesn't feel well or becomes depressed, they bring it into their relationships. People with low self-esteem can find it hard to build balanced relationships. It is not only because of their thinking errors but also because of how they attach to others. Relationships can be stigmatized by beliefs such as people should like me, I am not good enough, sacrifice yourself for others, and so on. These types of beliefs allow emotional availability and bounds to unhealthy relationships or toxic romances.

Someone lacking self-admiration or pride becomes vulnerable to be victimized or manipulated. Improvement of self-esteem helps better control affection. Consciously dealing with unhealthy relationships means carefully choosing people and emotionally detaching from wrongdoers. It doesn't mean that people give up on others, but it is important to monitor relationships with well-being in mind. Like attracts like, so connect with like-minded people. People have to acknowledge that they have to watch their own bounds and feelings (they can't control the feelings of others).

Imbalanced relationships are stressful, especially if they are with family members or bosses. They can knock down self-esteem. The number one rule in fixing imbalanced relationships is setting and maintaining clear boundaries; firmly set limits defining points of control. Relationships become better when individuals understand their position.

Even in close relationships, people can decide how much they want to offer. Personal involvement in the life of others is a choice. People decide how much time they spend with others, what topics they share or how much emotional involvement they give out. They can also control how and why they think about others. Having unrealistic expectations and the wrong understanding of relationships always cause problems.

People can decide to respond differently and they can do so without eroding self-esteem. They must be aware of how their relationships contribute to self-esteem. With the application of previously discussed rights and new beliefs, they become more competent. They choose topics of conversation, excuse themselves from uncomfortable situations, exercise respect, choose words and body language sensibly, practise non-reactive responses, open up to constructive criticism, filter emotional reasoning, etc. By now, you have a chunk of good knowledge you have to apply.

I am initiative in relationships. I care how I contribute to relationships. I learn to set and maintain boundaries. I improve my beliefs. I understand my position in relationships. I clarify and maintain boundaries. I understand what I control in a relationship. My opinions and actions matter a great deal. I monitor self-expression. I don't avoid disagreements. I am assertive. I am fair to myself and others. I don't focus on negativity but on facts. I control my emotional involvement.

Confident Me

write here
write NOW

You should reflect your relationships and apply knowledge from previous relationships. You can write about troubled relationships and identify the points of their problems. Your task is to find your points of control and what you can do (not the other party) to fix it. You also have to acknowledge that some relationships can be very toxic and unrepairable. Sometimes the end of a relationship is the only option to protect oneself. For instance, abusive relationships need much more than the reader's work.

Writing about my relationships:

Actions to fix imbalanced relationships:

Actions to build fruitful relationships:

CHAPTER 7

Some people might think of compassion as something related to religion or spirituality. As a matter of fact, compassion is a beautiful and frequently overlooked human quality. It is like offering help to someone who suffers. Bringing kindness and gentleness to oneself is delivering the type of feelings that people generally miss and long for. In the next practice, you will learn to use compassion and kindness to generate good feelings while enforcing solid self-esteem built upon good qualities.

7.1 SELF-COMPASSION

Compassion is a strong antidote to negativity. It helps in situations when people act for protection or excitement. These situations might be real or imagined threats (previously discussed false alarm). When people feel a threat, their bodily reactions and thinking change. When actions are fired by excitement, this again affects thinking and bodily responses. Acting in protection and excitement often makes people exhibit undesirable emotions and behaviour. When people are emotionally reactive, things often get worse. To make things better, people need a calm and non-reactive response. Compassion is to train a person to behave and feel calm. Compassion halts reacting when one may detect (false) danger. It also teaches to correct one's emotional reactions and behaviour.

Similar to empathy, compassion is an emotional experience and response to feelings. Also, it includes the intention to help. When people notice the suffering of their loved ones, they become compassionate and want to help. But when they suffer, they react differently. They become more harsh and self-critical. They tend to be emotionally reactive and things often get worse. To stop this, you will try self-compassion. Instead of beating yourself up when you suffer, you will practise self-compassion. Self-compassion is not easy and it is to bring loving care and good feelings towards oneself.

People might resist self-compassion because they are conditioned to be critical. They don't want to fail, make or repeat mistakes, so they criticize. Also, because they want to protect others and be better for others, they might think that criticism is what they need. Self-criticism may come from well-meaning or as motivation to do better but it can make things worse. When people go through difficulties or the consequences of their mistakes are dramatic, the criticism just adds to all the negativity. Practice of compassion removes criticism and judgement when they are not needed.

Exercising self-compassion enhances self-worthiness and self-love. Along with the practice of appreciation and receiving compliments, you can deliver positive messages to yourself. You make yourself valuable. With making compassion and kindness one of your own qualities, your self-esteem rises. When things don't work out as you wish, you will activate compassion instead of berating yourself. Self-compassion means to be empathetic and offer the kind assistance to oneself. Compassion also aids emotional flexibility. When you are emotionally resilient, you more efficiently respond to difficulties. Instead of reacting at difficult times, you take responsibility and compassionately help.

I learn and practise self-compassion. If for whatever reasons I don't do well, I don't beat myself up. I deal with the consequences with self-compassion. I allow self-compassion in difficulties. It helps me to develop self-love. When I am hurt, I don't need self-criticism. I need kindness and help. I practise self-compassion to allow healing. I also practise compassion to help others when they need it.

You can listen to guided imagery "Let Go of the Past". The password is "emotions" without the quotes.

Confident Me

write here
write NOW

Positive response to the previous section:

Situations I need self-compassion for:

Situations that I can offer compassion:

7.2 SHIFTING YOUR FIXATION

In this part, you will learn that letting go of the past can be easier than one might think. Once realizing that memory behaves oddly and perhaps is not reliable, people find more reasons not to dwell on the past.

Memory can be seen like a filing cabinet that stores files. When people pull a file from their memory to awareness, they activate thoughts and emotions. While doing this, they add new thoughts and emotions to a story. (In the same way that people can add a few notes into an office file). They push this new version into their unconsciousness and next time they recall the last version of their story. (The same as they would pull an office file with the notes.) Reliability of past stories can be based on how many times they were retrieved into awareness.

Files from a filing cabinet can be modified or destroyed, just like memory files can. They have to be pulled into awareness and intentionally changed. With some imagination, people can destroy bad files, rewrite or create new memory files. This new understanding is used by professionals, for example, in psychiatry or by psychotherapists to treat trauma.

Emotionally painful memories can erode self-esteem, and they should be dealt with through self-compassion. One can be too negative about the future because of what they experienced. People with low self-esteem irrationally tend to blame themselves and an aching memory can just maintain this tendency. Sometimes they believe in deserved punishment for wrongdoing. Whether they experienced disappointments, betrayals, rejections or failures, they can be lost in their thinking and feelings. Dwelling on something painful doesn't serve well for anyone.

People can bring compassion and kindness to overcome the past hurts. Once they start believing in their worthiness, they acknowledge wasteful energy given to the past that can't be changed. With compassion and kindness, people can bring a new light into their interpretation of the past. With care, they can dispute their thoughts and ask how their memory contributes to self-esteem. They remember compassion is the ability to feel and desire to help. They are willing to re-write memory files with compassion and kindness.

I can let go of my negative past. I can intentionally bring my negative stories to awareness. I can bring compassion and kindness to my memory. I can bring closure to my past with kindness and compassion. I am working hard to improve my self-esteem. I can't allow the past stories to ruin it. I deserve to feel well.

write here / write NOW In response to the previous section, choose one of your negative experiences you wish to let go of. With compassion and kindness, write a new interpretation of your story. You can do it a few times until your story is believable. Remember you are not going to change the facts you remember. You try to make a new interpretation based on a changed understanding and with balanced thinking.

My story:

Positive thoughts about the previous paragraphs:

7.3 THERAPEUTIC FOCUS

Just like people help their friends by guiding them, they can help themselves by self-coaching. Goals motivate and help to stick in the right direction. They can be used to give meanings and satisfaction. They can be checkpoints and help to return on the right path when drifting away. Small goals cover achievements within days or a month. Long-term goals plan achievements within a year. Lifetime goals can reflect personal philosophy and values. Goals should complement each other to harmonize achievements. Small goals are strategies towards bigger goals.

Goals not only help to stop fiddling around but also, they give feelings of fulfilment which is necessary for self-esteem. When people have purpose expressed through simple goals, they maintain their focus and follow through. Achievement of personal goals increases self-worthiness as people more often feel well and they acknowledge their deeds.

Small goals can be ideal to target positive feelings about oneself or help to maintain self-esteem. People are better driven when they have meaning. Self-esteem reinforces when people are recognized. Small goals can be a strategy to remember self-recognition. A goal like "Today I will thank myself each time I do something for others" is simple and easily achievable. For example, to meet this goal, a person just thanks themselves when they pass something to others, let another person goes first, finish their report on time, drop children off at school, offer coffee to their partner, lend a pen to a co-worker, and so on. Those are little things people do daily yet, they stay unnoticed.

Another example of a simple goal might be "This week every day at lunchtime I will practise five minutes of mindful walking". It is easy and achievable. This doesn't depend on anything or anybody and once it's achieved, a person acknowledges the easiness of achieving. Once people manage to set a correct goal and stick to their intention overtime it becomes super-easy. They don't have to put too much effort into maintaining correct focus.

Sometimes people have to be flexible in order to respond to what happens and adapt their goals. Life always brings surprises and new circumstances which can change priorities. Although the goals are created with an intention of their achievements, some level of adaptability helps. Sometimes new circumstances move towards the goals, while other times they may have an opposite effect. Adjustment of personal goals might be necessary.

When I create personal goals, I consider my feelings. I can create goals to improve how I feel about me. Goals help me to stay in control and focused. I can prioritize self-esteem in small goals. I choose where I put my thoughts and feelings. With patience, I redirect my focus on what I intend to do.

---

write here / write NOW

Here, you create small, daily goals that will target improvement of self-esteem. Timely, you will assess their achievements. Also, underneath each goal, you write how you will praise yourself upon achievements. If you for whatever reasons don't meet your goal, you will try to do it the following day and move all goals one day forward. Thus, you have to achieve your goals in chronological order.

My small goal for tomorrow:

When I meet this goal this is what I will tell myself:

My small goal for the day after tomorrow:

When I meet this goal, this is what I will tell myself:

My small goal to be achieved in three days:

When I meet this goal this is what I will tell myself:

You can continue creating and meeting personal goals. In the future, you can target various aspects of personal development, unnecessary and dysfunctional beliefs. You can aim for an improvement of communication, assertive behaviour, good qualities, self-admiration or any other aspects that might be difficult to develop. It is important to remember that goals have to be smart: specific, measurable, achievable, realistic and have time specification.

CHAPTER 8

As you know, having low esteem makes many things difficult, from blaming yourself for things that aren't your fault to underestimating personal values, from missing self-love to feeling ashamed. People might be over-sensitive, over-reactive or over-analytical. Having balanced thinking and taking beneficial actions are critical to maintain solid self-esteem, along with that, people have to value their feelings.

8.1 THROUGH THOUGHTS AND FEELINGS

Feelings and emotions are a vital life experience and you can learn more about them in the future. In this section, you will get a brief inside into regarding emotions. Valuing feelings is not difficult when one feels positive emotions but it's dissimilar when someone feels resentment or unhappiness, or any other negative emotions. People every so often don't know what to do with anger, sadness or frustration. Because they are not pleasant and people associate negative emotions with events or people who they would rather forget, they avoid them. They might think negative feelings are unwanted reminders (and indeed they are).

Avoidance could be effective short-term help. As the time passes, people forget and don't have to worry. However, if the reasons for negative feelings don't change, avoidance doesn't work. People suppress emotions but they come back. They do it again and again, but because the problem is unresolved, the feelings creep back. Attempts to banish bad feelings can be a trap. Avoiding feelings turns into stressful vigilance.

Negative feelings might be like a snowball rolling down a steep hill covered with snow. As the ball rolls, it becomes larger and rolls faster. When emotions snowball, they become more complex and difficult to manage.

People can learn to better understand emotions. Negative feelings can provide feedback when something goes wrong. They might bring attention to an issue that should be resolved. Avoiding negative feelings also could mean blindfolding; when a person doesn't want to know or denies the truth. Feelings posed by rejecting the truth can obstruct self-esteem. Acknowledging the truth might be painful but it can help to resolve a problem. In the long run, knowing the truth is positive. It can stop a cycle and prevent wrong actions or choices from taking place. If feeling negative emotions, people should be curious. They should try to understand why they feel what they feel.

People with low self-esteem often experience guilt. These chapters already talked about it and hopefully you started distinguishing between imagined and real guilt. At this point, it's beneficial to remember that guilt relates to actions. It is feedback letting you know that something was done wrong and against values. Guilt should prompt people to different actions in the future. People have to deal with consequences and prevent acting against their values again. Sometimes guilt can be compensated by fixing consequences. Guilt should stop when actions have been corrected. One finding hard to let go of irrational guilt should use compassion and forgiveness to move on.

I pay attention to my feelings. I might resist recognizing the truth when I deny my feelings. When noticing that I feel negative emotions, I am curious. I try to identify the causes. When I feel worthless I try to understand why and what I have to change to feel differently. Sometimes I might not know the reasons for my feelings, so I just accept them. If I don't know why I feel what I feel, I stay interested. Doing this helps to understand and make corrections. Acknowledging feelings helps me to better understand myself.

---

write here / write NOW — You should focus on your own feelings and perhaps try to identify the meanings of your recurring negative feelings (if there are some). Sometimes the reasons of negative feelings are well hidden and you can just accept them (it is what it is). Maybe in the future you will understand better.

Refection on the previous paragraphs:

Actions to manage feelings:

8.2 BEING NON-JUDGEMENTAL

From childhood on, people are encouraged to be judgemental and have opinions but sometimes judgemental thinking can be more harmful than useful. People might rush with opinions and let judgements grow into beliefs. They could be trapped in negativity because of their judgemental thinking. In this section, you will learn about being non-judgemental to maintain self-esteem.

Non-judgemental thinking is not easy but people can learn it and benefit from it. Not judging is the opposite to what people do in modern life. People are used to judging almost anything and anywhere. Judgements can turn into harsh criticism (and self-criticism). Self-judgements can be cruel and people might be too quick to criticise. Sometimes they stubbornly preserve judgements and do it at the cost of eroding their self-esteem.

People don't have to see a silver lining where it isn't. They can learn to acknowledge that not everything is black and white, good or bad, right or wrong. They can afford not to have opinions (as already mentioned in the rights people have). At times, the best is just recognizing things as they are. People can just notice without giving any attributes. There's nothing wrong with seeing and naming things as they are.

I don't have to be judgemental. Perhaps I am not always aware of my judgements. I want to pay attention when I am conclusive about myself. Sometimes I have to be reminded it is better to stay neutral than critical. I can let get go of self-serving judgements. I can practise open-mindedness.

 You can practise guided imagery "Acceptance". The password is "emotions" without the quotes.

The following technique intentionally teaches non-judgemental thinking. You can practise it daily and gradually develop a less judgemental attitude. Every day, you can choose one thing you want to be non-judgemental about. Cultivating a non-judgemental attitude gradually re-frames unconstructive thinking such as black and white thinking, emotional filtering and reasoning, dwelling or ruminating.

---

write here — You can apply this five step technique to a specific judgement about yourself.

1. Chose a judgement
2. Write the reasons for letting go of it. Accept the reasons.
3. Replace the judgements with facts.
4. Create a non-judgemental statement that can replace the judgement.
5. Describe the impacts of a non-judgemental statement

Positive reactions to non-judgemental stance:

When people experience rejections, disappointments, betrayals, failures or make mistakes, they tend to be self-judgemental. They forget to focus on all aspects of that experience. Non-judgemental thinking helps to remove emotional involvement. It allows finding a way around it. When people experience situations that attack self-esteem, they can try to neutrally recognize them as they are. This allows paying attention to acceptance. A non-judgemental attitude allows compassion and self-compassion. People can develop a habit of paying attention to impact their judgements. Self-induced negativity and rejection can grow from self-judgemental (unjustified) thinking. A negative attitude never helps and looking at problems in bigger views needs balanced thinking.

Experiencing losses is part of life. Often, losses get people unprepared. Accepting losses might take time. Recovering from losses, especially losses of significant relationships, can be difficult. Losses come with questions and people try to understand why someone left them or betrayed them. Low self-esteem can make people irrationally blame themselves, and they turn too self-critical. At this point, however, criticism is the last thing they need. They already suffer from a loss and they need kindness and compassion. Sometimes it's better not to try to understand why someone left or treated a person badly. Human actions can be unpredictable, complicated and not always understood.

You should acknowledge that at times of losses you have to put energy into learning how to live after a loss. Non-critical thinking and trust that time will help should replace self-blame or guilt. People have to allow living with that loss and believe that over time they can be happy again. Losses may leave big gaps and it's good to fill them with meaningful actions. A loss always has two sides and they have to be noticed.

Confident Me

> *I avoid being overly critical. I try to catch self-criticism. I replace it with a non-judgemental attitude. I practise putting things in a bigger perspective. I acknowledge when doing wrong. I focus on improving in the future. When I suffer, I remember self-compassion.*

write here
write NOW

Actions to practise non-judgemental stance:

CHAPTER 9

learning new strategies

Although people don't have a full understanding of the mind and brain, they can learn to use them for personal benefits. The mind and brain together can do a lot of good work for self-esteem. The following paragraphs discuss a few strategies of using the brain and mind to improve self-esteem.

You can can find additional information.

In the following parts, you will learn about visualization and mindfulness. Mindfulness is awareness and people can learn it quite easily and at any age. Mindfulness means to experience the present moment and be aware. Awareness starts with paying attention to thoughts and feelings in the moment. It also involves paying attention to surroundings.

Mindfulness can beautifully help people to improve self-esteem. Mindfulness and visualization relate to the brain's activities. It is helpful when you know a bit about the theory behind them.

The brain is made up of billions of cells called neurons and they pass information by electric activities. With the use of sensitive equipment (EEG), professionals found these electric activities are cyclic and they create patterns. The patterns, impacting the whole body, change based on physical and mental activities of an individual.

For instance, during waking hours, the brain produces high-frequency brainwaves called gamma and during the state of deep sleep, a low frequency called delta. There is a range of brainwaves between gamma and delta and each of them have profound effects. They can also tell much about the health of a person. For example, people suffering with Attention Deficit Disorder (ADD) lack beta brainwaves. People suffering with Anxiety Disorders have an abundance of beta waves.

Remember that by changing mental and physical activities you can impact your brain's electric activities. When just closing their eyes, people reduce stimulations and their brain changes the frequency of brainwaves. By changing electric activities, the brain produces different chemicals. For example, during sleep, relaxation and meditation, the brain produces natural chemicals called endorphins (beta-endorphins, dopamine). These chemicals are important for good feelings and they are beyond enlarged mental clarity (when the right side of the brain creates images). These feelings can last for hours or days.

People can intentionally help their brain to produce these good chemicals. When they do it regularly, their brain adapts and responds faster and the effects can last longer. In relaxation and meditation, people can activate a state as just before falling asleep (alpha brainwaves) or activate deep relaxation just as light sleep (theta brainwaves). Those are the states when their brain doesn't process much information while it is still receptive and absorbent. Practically, people interrupt the electric cycles and allow the brain to do "different jobs". This can be hugely beneficial, especially on busy days, when stressed, when people are overstimulated, restless, lack restorative sleep or just feel unwell.

Example

You can do one of the following experiments:

1 Think about a person you love or profoundly like. Close your eyes and think about why and what you love about them, about good times you spend together, and remember the feelings you get when you are around them. Imagine their face; notice beautiful details you like. Imagine their smell, voice, touch or taste. Think about them for about five minutes. When you finish, observe what it did to your feelings and body.

2 Think about a situation that made you very happy. Close your eyes and think profoundly about it. Imagine the details of that situation. Visualize yourself in details and exactly what you were doing, clothes you were wearing, how you were feeling, the whole surrounding where it happened, people, details of the place, colours, objects, smells, words and sounds, maybe even taste. Try to employ your senses. Imagine what you smelled and what sounds were connected to it. Think about them for about five minutes. When you finish, observe what it did to your feelings and body.

9.1 USING VISUALIZATION

The previous examples illustrated how people can consciously impact their body and feelings. They can use abilities to improve self-esteem. Imagination is enabled by a neural network which spreads across large areas of the brain. This triggers so-called associations and reactions in the body.

There is no substantial difference between what happens in the body when people have a real-life experience and when they imagine things. The brain and body respond similarly to imaginative and real.

People can visualize almost anything they want. They can imagine objects, situations or ideas and even experience certain feelings, and they do it. They visualize something they have never seen. They use imagination in creation, invention or resolving problems. They use imagination when they plan or remember. Unintentionally, they might imagine something fearful, bad or tragic. They might imagine something pleasant, holidays or dream places. All these can impact feelings. Because of the brain and bodily reactions to what people visualize, this is intentionally used in arts, marketing or sports. The difference between unintentional and intended visualization is that people deliberately create images to change their feelings and behaviour, to motivate or make people believe. For example, when athletes want to believe that they can win, they imagine details of winning actions.

I can practise visualization to enhance self-esteem. My imagination can positively influence self-esteem. I can practise intentional imagination to relax and feel well. I can visualize that my self-esteem is growing. I can imagine feeling confident. My imagination can be limitless.

A technique called mental imagery can be used to reduce stress, to strengthen positive emotions, let go of negative feelings, etc. It can be used in pain management, alternating thoughts or dealing with fear and anxiety, and also to help self-esteem. When using imagination, people experience so-called psychological time or mental travelling; they physically don't change but mentally move somewhere else. This technique involves the whole body and senses; similarly to when people are absorbed in activities or they daydream. The mechanism of mental imagery relates to how the two sides of the brain process information. The left side of the brain thinks logically and processes sequentially. The right side thinks in pictures and processes simultaneously. The left side is more attuned to the outside world while the right side to the inner world and emotions.

Examples

Visualization to calm
People can calm with the phrase "I am feeling calm". To start with, they focus on its meaning and effect. They try to think about nothing but the phrase. Softly, they whisper the phrase over like a broken record. They can close their eyes and do it for about three to five minutes.

Visualization to relax body
Autogenic instructions can be used to relax the body. Simply people imagine a part of the body they instruct and imagine it becomes relaxed. They can relax the whole body and start by instructing, such as, "The muscles on my face are relaxed" and imagine they soften and relax. Then imagine their neck and say, "My neck feels relaxed". They imagine their neck relaxing. They shouldn't rush and after imagining each part, they focus on their relaxed feelings before they move to another part. This way, they can move throughout the whole body: shoulders, chest, back, arms, abdomen, legs, and feet. This practice can take about five minutes.

Visualization to let go of disturbing or negative thoughts

People can visualize their thoughts as a dark cloud above their head. They can patiently imagine the darkness detaching and moving away, taking all disturbing thoughts and feelings away. They imagine each exhale pushes the cloud away until it floats in the sky. It carries away thoughts until they disappear. The empty space left after the removed thoughts can be filled with positive thoughts. They can be specific and target self-esteem, for example: I am worthy. I have good qualities that make me proud. This is what I appreciate about me_. I accept myself as I am.

Visualization to give up negative emotions

People can imagine a negative emotion as dark clouds. When they feel fear, they can imagine a dark cloud in their head. If they feel sad, they can imagine it around their heart. If they feel angry, the dark cloud could be around the stomach area. They then let go of the cloud merged in the sky. The gap left can be filled with good feelings, for instance, feeling satisfied, cheerful, confident, courageous, passionate, caring, brave, etc.

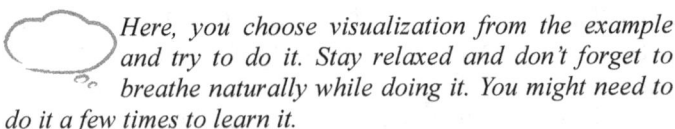

Here, you choose visualization from the example and try to do it. Stay relaxed and don't forget to breathe naturally while doing it. You might need to do it a few times to learn it.

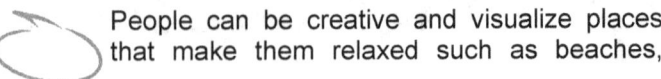

People can be creative and visualize places that make them relaxed such as beaches, meadows, mountains, lakes, seas or rivers. They can close their eyes and hold the desired images with all details, hear the sounds and smell the scents.

Practise of visualization should be done in a private comfortable place. Using visualization to raise self-esteem the reader can focus on aspects of self-esteem they want to improve. They can visualize letting go of negative beliefs that block them. They can identify specific feelings by imagining them as bright light entering their body, letting the feelings penetrate every cell of their body. Changing negative thoughts could be done by imagining them as specific images leaving their body and merging with the air. You can be creative and playful and use visualization for their benefits.

Scan here to practise "Guided Mental Imagery". The password is "emotions" without the quotes.

Reaction to previous:

Action to use visualization to improve self-esteem:

9.2 MINDUFLNESS TO RAISE SELF-ESTEEM

People with low self-esteem hold onto their stories and sometimes fixate on negatives for too long. They remove their attention from what they do, think about their actions or worry about something in future. They are mentally not present. Practicing mindfulness is to be fully involved in whatever people do; be in the present moment with full attention and with all senses. This increases awareness and people worry less and stop questioning their actions or appearance.

Building mindfulness happens through the connection of the mind, feelings and actions. While recognizing what happens, people are aware of how it affects whatever they experience. Mindfulness simply deepens experiences. Mindfulness is a skill that builds and improves with practise.

I can learn mindfulness. I can improve my self-esteem when doing things with full awareness. I pay attention to the present. When I do things mindfully, I can't worry or criticize myself. Over time, I can do mindfulness naturally and easily.

People can build mindfulness through curiosity and focus. Curiosity is important and adults sometimes forget it. They do a lot of things without noticing, automatically and with low engagement. When they become curious about the things they must bring attention to, they can look at the things and themselves differently when they are interested. Curiosity allows noticing what might be overlooked and recognizing good things that stay unnoticed.

You can learn formal mindfulness (called meditation). It is done by sitting in a quiet place and bringing attention to your internal world, thoughts and feelings. Meditation comes with non-judgemental noticing of what happens within a person. This helps you to stay grounded and accept. Formal mindfulness can improve feelings about oneself, and perhaps people can have a spiritual experience.

In meditation, people experience a state of the unfocused, floating or passive mind. It can be frequently filled with shifting images. Practising mindfulness can be a personal goal targeting self-esteem. Learning formal mindfulness is simple and starts with sitting for a few minutes in quietness and with closed eyes. It's literally doing nothing, which some people can find strange. While doing it, people don't assume any experience or force any mental activities. They just attend to what happens within them. Over time, people build comfort in silence and increased awareness. They can attend to breathing and gradually stop noticing the breath. You are advised (if you haven't started yet) to develop this skill.

I find meditation easy. I don't expect much to happen. I do it with my non-judgemental mind. I am patient. I can tolerate doing nothing. When I close my eyes, I notice my breath. I can hear it. I attend to my thoughts and emotions. I notice how my body feels. I don't try to control my thoughts. I don't judge. I try not to engage in thinking. I just learn to let the thoughts come and go. I don't hold on to my thoughts. I sit quietly daily for at least five minutes.

 You can learn more about mindfulness in daily life.

Comment to previous section:

Actions to take to practise mindfulness:

CHAPTER 10

Maintaining self-esteem includes good feelings about the appearance and body. Taking care of the body, eating healthy and be active always help. People might experience self-rejection when they focus only on the sides they don't like. Pondering on negatives is a thinking error that maintains a wrong attitude. When people learn to balance their thinking, they start noticing what they overlooked. By remembering to recognize the good qualities, they gain better control of how they feel.

10.1 TOWARDS SELF-ACCEPTANCE

At times, for whatever reasons, people fight against things that are out of their control. People with low self-esteem might be focused on aspects of appearance that are natural limits. With acceptance and directing focus towards qualities they possess, they stop fighting against limitations. They use their energy for improving, whether weaknesses or the development of skills.

I am focused on what I impact. Knowing what I can change is important but it is not everything. I have to take correct actions. I am not wasting time trying to change what I can't change. I do things by improving and showing my qualities.

With improving self-esteem, people learn that their life might not be perfect and this has to be accepted. Just like people accept a place of birth, or the family they were born into, acceptance of personal limits is necessary. Some people are better than others at some things and that can result from natural limits. Comparison is not always necessary and beneficial. It can be damaging to self-esteem. People with low self-esteem tend to test their worthiness in experiences or successes. It erodes their self-esteem as success is not worthiness and can come from differences amongst people. People have to nurture the ability to accept instead of comparing or testing.

People with low self-esteem might hide or cover up what, in their judgement, is shameful or making them worthless. By now, you have learnt about being non-judgemental and should also be able to let go of irrational thoughts that trigger feelings of shame, or tendencies to hide imperfections. Acceptance is an additional step towards release from self-infused distress. Admitting or even talking about flaws can sound scary. What if someone won't like you then? You already know that "what if" is a thinking error and you can counteract by analyzing the risks.

When people accept that anyone and everyone has weak points, does something shameful, makes mistakes and has flaws, they stop focusing on their own. They can relax and stop censoring themselves. Self-acceptance doesn't mean only accepting personal minuses but also acknowledging and accepting personal pluses. In real life, it means that people can feel well about themselves regardless. Everything becomes easier when people accept.

Self-acceptance opens the gate for self-admiration and self-love. It increases confidence and trust. People are not dragged down when they make mistakes; they accept them. People focus on building stability and being resistant against negativity. They recognize that they deserve good things even if they make mistakes and have flaws. They stop measuring events by how valuable people are.

Confident Me

write here / write NOW — Focus on your pluses and minus, strengths and weaknesses. You will make a list of pluses and minuses. Then you will thoroughly review the lists and try to recognize which ones are difficult to accept. Remember to fairly measure and accept also your pluses (not overlook or diminish them).

List of pluses:

List of minuses:

List of what I have to accept:

Action to take to accept:

10.2 GROWING CONFIDENCE

Confidence is not a personality trait as sometimes people believe. Confidence is a component of self-esteem that comes from thinking and beliefs. It grows from a belief that a person is capable of doing something. Based on beliefs, people create feelings about their abilities, tasks, roles or functions. People can feel confident about them or not.

Confidence is very important and influential. It is not only about knowledge and skills but also confidence that reduces or increases one's performance. People lose confidence when they stop believing in their abilities. Sometimes people are confident in one area and less confident in another. Confidence strengthens with practise and increased knowledge. Positive thinking and encouraging beliefs improve confidence.

Confident people don't think of mistakes as problems, but rather as learning opportunities. They choose and learn from confident people. They let their confidence "rub off on them". After people become more confident, they offer advice and help. When confident people become role models, their confidence strengthens. Low confidence can be maintained by thinking errors and a negative attitude.

Confidence can be influenced by factors such as unhappiness, lack of preparation or knowledge, poor time management, missing skills or a negative experience. People with low self-esteem generally lack confidence. Sometimes they are confident in specific areas. Building confidence takes practice and relates to a willingness to learn.

My beliefs impact my confidence. I may hold onto some beliefs that undermine my confidence. I want to know what I can do to improve confidence. If I lack confidence, I am prone to make mistakes. I want to feel confident.

Confidence improves through learning, problem solving and decision-making. Naturally, people feel less confident about the unknown, new or potentially difficult circumstances. Nothing else can help more than a positive mindset. Planning and preparation are good strategies to lessen the impact of the unknown. Once people are prepared, their confidence increases.

Achievements and some level of competence reinforce confidence. It may take time to develop confidence but working with beliefs in personal competence always speeds it up. Through positive beliefs, people express a willingness to dedicate and have discipline. Confidence develops a desire to improve along with the process of accomplishment.

Once a person achieves confidence, it will be great for their self-esteem. Learning and developing new skills are opportunities to accomplish something new which enhances positive beliefs in personal capacities. The basic rules are to highlight strengths, learn from mistakes and work towards improvement. Positive attitude allows focusing on confident progress.

I am building confidence. I trust in my potential. I can be resourceful, creative and determined. I do things to improve my confidence. I build habits of taking actions. I set personal goals. I know my strengths and weaknesses. I monitor and correct beliefs that undermine my confidence.

write here / write NOW — Once again, you should pay attention to your beliefs and how they may undermine confidence. It is important to acknowledge that confidence is not fixed and can change.

Beliefs that undermine confidence:

Actions to change them:

Beliefs that raise confidence:

Actions to demonstrate confidence:

Sometimes people take a second person's perspective to judge the impact they have on others. They do it in front of mirrors or in real social interactions. People want to be aware of what to do and not to do to impact others. Having this perspective is a useful reflection that helps to correct if something is wrong. Judging oneself with the eyes of others is better done comfortably and privately. In real social situations, it can be disruptive. It disturbs attention and decreases concentration. People can become too focused on how they impact others that they shift their attention on feelings instead of more important things. Mindfulness and assertive communication in real life helps to prevent it.

You already learned about the importance of body language. Because the body language not only sends messages but also affects feelings and moods (moods are prevailing emotions over some time), remember to apply your knowledge. By holding straight postures, sitting or walking, people send messages of confidence and increase confident feelings. Looking down can signal submission or avoiding eye contact might be read as shyness or guilt. By keeping the head straight, eyes levelled and shoulders back, a person signalizes assertiveness and positivity. Meeting someone's gaze can signal respect, interest, and depending on the context of the body language, can massage invitation or attraction.

By body language, people can tell the differences between positive reactions and rejections. Postures can convey a lot about someone's emotional and mental state, or information about the availability of that person. They can show a willingness to communicate. Positive messages and openness are signalled by a smile, gentle nodding, direct gaze and a straight posture. Keeping attention on the other person means people want their attention. By keeping attention on oneself, they keep other people's attention out.

I practise body language. I control what messages I send through my body talk. I am aware of where my attention goes. When I am nervous, I use breathing techniques to relax. I watch how I feel and what messages I send. I practise mindfulness.

Continue to allow good feelings by listening to "Allow Good Feelings". The password is "emotions" without the quotes.

Confident Me

write here / write NOW — Summarize your understanding and application of body language to improve confidence and self-esteem. Through actions, you can include small, personal goals, goals of developing new skills, and learning something new. It can be just improving assertive behaviour, mindfulness or relaxation.

Response to previous part:

Actions to do:

CHAPTER 11

Daily, people make a variety of decisions; some are important and others are trivial. They make around ten thousand choices every day. Low self-esteem doesn't help and choices can be confusing, making people anxious. Once decisions and choices are done, they close the door on other possibilities. Often, low self-esteem makes people indecisive. They worry about making a wrong choice and they procrastinate. They doubt their decisions, and once they finally decide on something, they continue questioning it. They blame themselves when things don't go as expected. They dramatize wrong choices. The next paragraphs will help you optimize your decisions. You can learn strategies assisting to more balanced choices.

11.1 KNOW THE PRINCIPLES

You can prevent second-guessing, dwelling or doubting when you learn how to make decisions. You have already improved you thinking errors and this positively impacts your decision-making. Learning decision-balancing with the application of mindfulness can halt your further doubts once the decision is made.

The next example includes a few rules that are critical in order to decrease the chances of wrong decisions or making the wrong choices. You are asked to thoroughly read them and think about how much or how little they apply to you.

Example

- Clearly identify a problem.
- Examine the entire landscape instead of focusing on only the obvious.
- Consider opposing information. Seek out information that contradicts personal beliefs. Search for information that could prove the decision is wrong.
- When making critical choices and decision the worst possible scenario should be considered.
- Consultation with a better informed source might be necessary.
- Realistic time for decision-making can prevent failure.
- Think through a decision but over-thinking doesn't bring better decision. Over-thinking is more confusing than clarifying.
- Significant information may be found in details or hidden facts.
- Consider values, priorities, intuition and feelings. Intuition is not impulsiveness; impulsiveness is the emotional urge to do something or to meet an emotional impulse of the moment.
- The decision maker has to accept risks that they don't have full control when something unforeseen happens.
- Some decisions don't work out as expected. This doesn't mean that a decision maker did it wrong. Having mixed feelings often occurs when making decision and choices.
- Everyone makes wrong choices and decision at some point. Mistakes are the source of growth and learning.

Making decisions employs a person's commitment to act upon a course of decision. This can work well along with personal goals to accomplish something. Choices figure out what people want and don't want. They also mirror values and beliefs. Once a specific choice is done, it helps to use positive language to state it. Personal choices expressed in statements can be useful. For instance, based on my balanced decision, I made the best choice I could. I have decided to invest money with_.

I pay attention to my daily choices. I trust that I do the best decisions at the time. I apply the knowledge to decide accurately. When making crucial decisions, I write the possible outcomes. It can help to notice overlooked facts. I accept that decisions and choices always involve risks. Once I decide, I state my decision in positive words. Accepting that I don't have full control over outcomes prevents hesitancy and procrastination.

write here / write NOW — Think through your approach to decisiveness and apply the previously mentioned rules to improve it.

My decision-making approach:

Actions to improve decisiveness:

11.2 BALANCING YOUR DECISIONS

Decision making involves actions and sometimes it is necessary to change behaviour. When, for example, someone wants to improve their confidence, they have to be willing to learn and experiment with new actions. This also includes designating time, will-power, and building discipline. Changing behaviour is not an easy task. It is useful to find the reasons, costs and benefits of behavioural change. To have a correct mindset, people can evaluate consequences of not changing and changing. They can weigh costs of changing on one side and the benefits on the other side. To change, the scale needs to tip so the benefits outweigh the costs.

Example

In this example, you can experiment and weigh changing or not changing you behaviour and choices. For example, you might be considering joining a social club, talking to a neighbour, quitting smoking, starting dancing, etc.

People weigh costs and benefits and they ask: What do I lose and gain by continuing my current behaviour?

Benefits of changing	Benefits of not changing
Cost of changing	Cost of not changing

To weigh it up, they can also consider the good things and less good things about changing.

Good things about not changing	Less good things about not changing
Less good things about changing	Good things about changing

Confident Me

I can improve when making balanced decisions. I weigh costs and benefits; the gains and losses. I think through. I consider risks involved in changes.

---

write here / write NOW — Choose a small but specific decision you have to do and weigh up the costs and benefits.

Decision I have to make:

Benefits of changing   Benefits of not changing

Costs of changing   Costs of not changing

Good things about not changing   Less good things about not changing

Less good things about changing   Good things about changing

11.3 AREAS OF HAPPINESS

Self-esteem narrowly relates to how people feel when satisfied in different areas of their life. Identifying fulfilment in these areas can be useful for self-reflection. This helps to direct the future focus on improvement of the less happy areas and increase self-esteem. The areas people focus on are: psychological well-being, physical health, family & home, social life & relationships, career (work), finances, interests and leisure.

In the next writing, you will rate your current satisfaction to better understand the next step you have to take. If, for example, someone is not happy with their physical health, by identifying the problems, they will be able to improve this when setting smart goals (specific, measurable, achievable, realistic, time). They can be creative and identify the potential improvement in each area. Throughout this practice, put together what you have learnt so far. You can use this point to review previous chapters and implement your knowledge. If someone finds this section challenging, they can simply create small (daily) goals for each area. These will be easy to monitor and used for learning. In the future they can review this part and practise.

 Each area is equally influential and people can assess using a scale of 1-10 while 1 is unsatisfied and 10 satisfied.

Psychological well-being:
Physical health:
Family & home:
Social life & relationships:
Career & work:
Finances:
Interests & leisure:

I create small daily goals to experience achievements. When I achieve, I build confidence. I focus on the less fulfilled areas of my life and improve them. When I don't achieve, I don't beat myself up. I can try to achieve again. I realistically take into account the circumstances and what works against my ambitions. I stay mindful and compassionate.

Once you clarify and set the goals, focus on the process of achievement. You must remember compassion and kindness can help overcome dissatisfaction. You mustn't forget self-appreciation and forgiveness are important replacements of criticism and self-blame.

write here
write NOW

You should start with the areas with the lowest satisfaction and try to identify what they miss and why you are dissatisfied. Write a few anecdotes about specific areas of your life and why you feel unfulfilled:

The next is setting the goals to increase satisfaction. You can go back to the sections about the goals to get help.

My smart goals:

Psychological well-being:

Physical health:

Confident Me

Family & home:

Social life & relationships:

Career & work:

Interests:

Finances:

CHAPTER

12

maintain the positive mindset

One might be surprised by how much they eliminate pressure when consciously using their mind. A positive attitude includes acknowledging limits and identifying sources of possible control. Immediately, people can relax when finding they have a choice, thought from limited options. They don't want to see themselves as victims of limits. They want to positively respond and accept when it's out of their control or resolve when a solution is available. In the next parts, you will continue learning and practising mindfulness to deepen a positive attitude.

Learn more about mindfulness.

12.1 REMEMBER MINDFULNESS

Practising mindfulness improves concentration and it can change automatic thinking because people catch negative thoughts and immediately they can stop them. Mindfulness grows and cultivates through practise. Before people make it their habit, they may forget about mindfulness. To avoid this, they can use simple reminders, for instance, the words "be mindful" written on a sticky note or as a message on their screen-saver. As soon as a person realizes forgotten mindfulness, they redirect their attention to a current moment. They do it each time until it will be easier and automatic.

At stressful times, people might need to pause, take a few moments to allow mindfulness. They can use meditation to recollect their energy. The fruit of mindfulness is personal protection. It provides stability in times of turmoil. Through meditation, people can experience joy and peace found in daily life. They shouldn't focus on mindfulness itself but be less self-conscious and easy about it. When being fully present is difficult, people literally have to stop. They tell themselves "stop this and be mindful right now". They can adopt this instruction as a personal command they follow. Through mindfulness, people can establish new habits and routines. Making mindfulness essential in daily experiences requires effort and it always pays back.

There are many mundane things and activities people do automatically such as walking, driving, travelling or even talking to someone. Doing them mindfully can be personal training to have a new skill of mindfulness. Sometimes people practise mindfulness for a while and they stop doing it. They might be consumed by a busy life, halted by obstacles or anything that happens in life. Realizing that they stop being mindful should alert them. Bringing attention to the present moment and doing things mindfully again is the only way to respond.

I practise mindfulness. I can use reminders to stay mindful. I gently force my attention to a present moment. I use mindfulness to change feelings about myself. I can create personal instructions to remember mindfulness. Mindfulness can be my mindset. I do things mindfully.

Essentially, meditation can be seen as an internal almost intimate experience when a person non-judgementally attends to their inner world. Anyone can practise meditation as long as they can be patient and passive. The ability to meditate, as with any other skill, starts from the basics. People sit in silence and attend to themselves. With persistence, open-mindedness and curiosity, almost anybody can advance.

Hopefully, you have started with basic meditation and if not, it's time to start now. Low self-esteem and lack of self-acceptance change once practising silent mediation daily for about twenty days. People can have a simple goal such as sitting in silence and attending to their own body and mind for five minutes. This is a realistic goal for almost everyone. You can learn about what happens in your body and mind when you don't do anything. Over time, you learn not only to tolerate your thoughts and feelings without fighting them but also to start enjoying your moments.

Meditation improves stress response, reduces distress and increases good feelings. The regular practice improves self-acceptance and helps to develop a positive relationship with self. Perhaps people don't fully understand what happens during meditation, but once they learn it, it becomes their favourite routine. Sometimes what people experience during meditation can't be explained (people can be mysterious about it or try to find meanings).

Meditations can be passive or have specific goals during focused meditation. People can target personal well-being or global concerns for example. Focused meditation means that meditators aim some experience such as calmness, love, kindness or peace. In focused meditation, people use words or phrases.

Example

Once you learned silent meditation you can try focused

meditation. Here are some ideas you can use in focused meditation:

- **Self-esteem**: I love myself, I love and accept myself, I am loved, I feel good about myself, I like myself, I think positively about myself
- **Acceptance**: I accept myself, I accept my life, I accept my past, I accept my flaws, I accept the flaws of others, I accept limits, I am who I am
- **Trust**: I trust myself, I trust everything that comes in my life, I can handle difficulties, I can cope with challenges, I trust that better times can come, I do my best always, I trust that everyone does their best
- **Fear**: I am letting go of fear, I feel secure, I choose courage, I feel strong, I am brave, I can face difficulties
- **Sadness**: I am letting go of sadness, I am feeling balanced, I am choosing to let go of sadness
- **Worthiness**: I am worthy, I feel worthy
- **Forgiveness**: I forgive myself, I forgive _ (a person), I forgive _ (an event or mistake), I can be free of blame, I can be free of guilt
- **Anger**: I am letting go of my anger, I am in peace, I can be calm
- **Hurt**: Letting go of emotional pain, I am letting go of pain, I am free of hurt, I can feel loved
- **Peace and love**: Love to everyone, Peace and love in me, I feel loved, Love for everyone, Love is free, Peace and blessings to all

I meditate to improve my self-esteem. I try to find comfort in doing nothing. This helps me to learn about my body and mind. It teaches me to accept my thoughts and me as a person. The silence becomes more tolerable when I do it daily. Once I learn silent meditation, I can try focused meditation.

write here
write NOW

Reaction to previous section:

Actions to practise daily meditation:

12.2 REMAIN STRATEGIC

 Remember other strategies that help to strengthen your positive mindset:

- Use self-reflection on the things you do; do it non-judgementally, easily and as a second person who cares.
- Practise seeing yourself in a bigger picture and do it with care.
- Exercise gratitude and appreciation of small things.
- Create a gratitude list of what you are grateful for to prompt positive thinking.
- Recognize when you do and feel well.
- Remind yourself of personal qualities you possess.
- Write positive thoughts into words and give them a more tangible form.
- Create lists of things you would like to do.
- When feeling frustrated, identify the things you do by choice.
- Learn not to sweat over small stuff.
- When your schedule is stretched, value any little effort and minutes you deliver kindness to yourself.
- Hold constructive, internal conversations (thinking) when alone or doing mundane things.
- Distinguish when in your thinking you target flaws or mistakes and change it right away.

In the following paragraphs, you will find a few examples of functional and meaningful thinking. People can choose some of them and write them as personal statements. They can be used as daily a motto to address personal problems

Example

Constructive thinking when lacking self-acceptance: Even though

I sometimes feel low about myself, I accept myself. I remember that I must be in control of my thinking. My thoughts generate feelings. I want to feel good about myself. I accept myself. I accept my mistakes.

Constructive thinking when losing trust: Although I try, sometimes I don't trust. I can trust again when I change my thinking. I look at problems from a wider perspective. Also, I consciously choose actions to enhance trust.

Constructive thinking in self-devaluation: Sometimes I focus on what I miss and depreciate myself. I can't dwell on my flaws. I want to value myself. I think about myself with compassion and kindness. I create positive thoughts by acknowledging my values.

Constructive thinking in fear of failure: Regardless of my experience, I can succeed. If I failed in the past, I learn from it. Failures are learning opportunities. I focus on my strengths. My actions have an impact. The most important thing is to try. I can succeed.

Constructive thinking when feeling shame: Everyone has small secrets they might feel ashamed of. I don't have to feel ashamed. I positively think about myself. When I change how I think I can let go of irrational shame.

When I do something wrong or embarrassing I might be too harsh. When I focus only on negative aspects I am unconstructive. I have to change this. I don't want to be doubtful. I put extra effort to control my thinking. I am capable to face challenges. I have a strong positive attitude. I can be optimistic.

 You can practise guided mindfulness "Mindfulness in Breathing". The password is "emotions" without the quotes.

Positive response:

Actions to maintain a positive mindset:

CHAPTER

13

Psychologists consider self-esteem as a human need that is essential for survival (William Jones). They see it as the core of human adaptation (Ernest Becker) with its social aspects. Society fosters self-esteem and building self-esteem is about building beyond oneself; on equality amongst human beings. You have to remember that in order to maintain self-esteem, you always have to perceive yourself as a valuable member of society. Keeping self-esteem solid must represent an attitude built on good values and care shown towards oneself and others.

13.1 BACK TO SELF-ASSESSMENT

sum it up

Through previous pages, you were guided to absorb that every person is amazingly unique in many ways. You went through practices to understand what to do to improve self-esteem and do it. You practised self-reflection to bring self-concept in alignment with your actions. Because self-esteem evolves by validation and assessment, you have to stay on the journey you started. Once you have acquired solid self-esteem, it is easier to continue. The initial self-assessment provided you with a starting point. You are encouraged to re-take the self-assessment and see your progress. You should honestly answer the questions and recognize your advancement. Don't be alarmed by your scores. Remember, you are on the journey, and small yet steady progress can be the best. Just don't stop.

Questionnaire

1. Do you believe that building healthy self-esteem is in or out of your control?

   Yes, it is in my control   No, it is not in my control

2. How often do you believe in yourself?

   Most of time   Often   Occassionally   Rarely   Never

3. How often do you feel confident in your abilities?

   Most of time   Often   Occassionally   Rarely   Never

4. How often do you worry about what other people think about you?

   Most of time   Often   Occassionally   Rarely   Never

5. How often do you halt your expression of thoughts and feelings?

   Most of time   Often   Occassionally   Rarely   Never

6. How often do you feel hopelessness and fear of retaliation?

   Most of time   Often   Occassionally   Rarely   Never

7. How often can you find truth in criticism?

   Most of time   Often   Occassionally   Rarely   Never

8. How often can you focus on problem-solving?

   Most of time   Often   Occassionally   Rarely   Never

9. Do you worry of rejection or being alone?

   Yes   No

10. Do you worry of conflicts?

    Yes   No

11. Can you read the minds of others?

   Yes   No

12. Are you a perfectionist?

   Yes   No

13. Do you worry about disclosing your true feelings and thoughts?

   Yes   No

14. Do you believe you must help when others feel upset?

   Yes   No

15. Do you think you should be always in control of emotions?

   Yes   No

16. Do you think you should be always happy and desired?

   Yes   No

17. Do you think people should be as you expect them to be?

   Yes   No

18. Do you worry of failure?

   Yes   No

19. Is it wrong to get frustrated?

   Yes   No

20. Do you worry others would find your flaws?

   Yes   No

21. Are you sarcastic or cynical?

   Yes   No

check your self-esteem continued...

22. Do you want others to think you are perfect?

    Yes   No

23. Do you counterattack when others attack you?

    Yes   No

24. Do you think you should feel only positive emotions?

    Yes   No

25. Do you think problems are caused by others?

    Yes   No

26. Is your attitude respectful?

    Yes   No

27. Do you acknowledge other person's feelings?

    Yes   No

28. Do you express your feelings and thoughts?

    Yes   No

29. Can you find common grounds when someone disagrees with your ideas?

    Yes   No

30. Can you find common grounds when someone disagrees with your ideas?

    Yes   No

31. Do you believe everyone is accountable for their own feelings?

    Yes   No

13.2 DON'T FORGET

Maintaining self-esteem is the practice to genuinely enhance self-esteem. As you will continue preserving your self-esteem, you should always place unrealistic and negative thoughts into wider views. Also, nobody gets it right without patience and kindness. Even if you have small slips and let the negativity temporary take over, it's not the end of the world. You can regain balanced thinking to fill your solid self-esteem with positive feelings.

To recap, you shouldn't hesitate to review this book. In the future, use it as a quick reference, especially during difficult times. Self-esteem changes in response to what happens and erodes after losses, rejections, and disappointments. To monitor self-esteem, you should look into these pages once every three or four months. You will be reminded of the basics you learned and can take extra steps to preserve solid self-esteem.

Hopefully, you grasp how self-esteem contributes to your happiness, resilience and fulfilment. People with solid self-esteem are not perfect. They are realistic, humble and proud. They can acknowledge strengths, weaknesses and potential. People can admire, feel worthy, and be determined to grow. They recognize their values and all people's worth. They are confident and allow other people to flourish their confidence.

It seems appropriate to finish with the words of Mahatma Gandhi:

*"Carefully watch your thoughts, for they become your words.
Manage & watch your words, for they will become your actions.
Consider & judge your actions, for they have become your habits.
Acknowledge & watch your habits, for they shall become your values.
Understand & embrace your values, for they become your destiny."*

 You can learn more about the power of the mind with book The Strongest You

ABOUT THE AUTHOR

Now residing in Yorkshire, England, Ivana Straska (Szakal), M. A., a successful educator and mental health professional, brings inspiration and her unique style to help others. Writing her books with guided practice was inspired by her clients and personal challenges. Her vast experience encouraged her to develop a unique approach that any person can adopt.

Straska was born in Bratislava, Slovakia (the former Czechoslovakia) where she grew up, obtained her degrees and first work experience in adult education. With her family, she moved to Toronto, Canada and pursued her ambitions in mental health. She launched her private practice in Toronto in 2008 when she became a member of The Association of Registered Psychotherapists & Mental Health Professionals (O.A.C.C.P.P.), Dalton Associates, Psychological & Counselling Services in Ontario. Shortly after, she joined GTA Psychological Services and extended her private practice from Greater Toronto Area throughout Halton and Waterloo Regions. With the development of online services, she has been working with many individuals from all walks of life, both in Canada and around the world.

Her expressed purpose has always been to help people experience the greatest possible fulfilment in their lives and her work grew into her passion. Her qualifications are augmented in extensive experience in the fields of education, psychotherapy, cognitive and behavioural therapy, mindfulness and mental imagery, all of which enforce her professional credibility. She teaches people to understand their mind and feelings, how to change ways of thinking and take new actions. These are achievable goals for anyone who wants to create healthy feelings and have positive life experience.

Straska's first book "The Strongest You" explains how the automatic mode of the mind can cause a dysfunctional service. The book and audio tracks teach self-coaching of the mind towards positive transformation. The reader is carried forward while purposefully using her approach tailored to individual's circumstances.

In her second book, "Mindfulness, Breathe In – Breathe Out", Straska educates the reader on what to do to live mindfully and feel happier and more satisfied. She explains how a modern individual can benefit from mindfulness. She takes the reader through the practice of stages of mindfulness in ordinary days.

Her latest book, "Confident Me", helps people caught in the trap of low self-esteem. It takes them on the journey of building solid self-esteem. With this book, Straska guides the reader to understand and align the values of self-concept with their actions. She helps readers to stop thinking negatively and targeting their skills, abilities, qualities, strengths, appearance and characteristics. Through thinking and writing, she guides the reader towards self-acceptance and confidence. She provides comprehensive strategies to change the habits eroding self-esteem.

 Ivana International

www.ingramcontent.com/pod-product-compliance
Lightning Source LLC
Chambersburg PA
CBHW070145080526
44586CB00015B/1843